THE MAGIC SELL

THE MAGIC SELL

A Seven Step Approach
for Consumer Electronics

Stan Adler

HDL PUBLISHING COMPANY
Costa Mesa, California

HDL Books
are published by HDL Publishing Company,
a division of HDL Communications,
650 Town Center Drive, Costa Mesa, Ca 92626.

10 9 8 7 6 5 4 3 2 1

PRINTED IN THE UNITED STATES OF AMERICA

ISBN 0-937359-03-3

To my Mom and Dad,
who let me do anything I wanted to do,
and to Carol, Christy, and Jenny,
who made sure I did it.

Contents

General Introduction to the Avatar Business Series

The premise guiding the Avatar Business Series takes only a little from the original meaning of the word derived from Sanskrit, "**avatar**," defined as the "manifestation of a deity in human form." By the mid-nineteenth century, indeed, "avatar" meant manifestation of anything, period. We have chosen the name for a series of books on achievement in business and in facets of business processes for several reasons. First, it sounds "right." It has a nice ring to it. Second, it seems to suggest a theme in the realization of superior performance, no matter what the enterprise or setting. Namely, the "avatar" manifests something. We think this holds true to the range of exceptional results accomplished in business **by people**. In other words, the result of any organizational endeavor is simply a manifestation of the energies and creativity of the people in that enterprise. And in many books on the market and on the credenzas of executives everywhere, people always seem incidental to business success. That's nonsense. There's more to it.

Many readers of these books come away with a sense that the success works for someone else. One may learn how ABC Systems reduced its turnover or how XYZ Widgets reduced inventory, but one doesn't learn what Mary Kelso **did** on a Tuesday afternoon to make these results a fact. Nor do we learn what Jim Brader **does** on those visits to customers. That imbalance is what the Avatar Business Series seeks to redress.

Consider the Brooklyn Bridge. Now standing more than a century, it was the folly of two men, named Roebling, father and son, one of whom gave his life in the course of the project (and the other suffered lifetime paralysis). The bridge, of course, has been long finished and has inspired everything from great poetry to the grandest display of fireworks to celebrate its hundredth anniversary. But from another vantage the Brooklyn Bridge manifests the **aggregate effort** and force of will **of many people**. We admire the product in its final form, having overlooked what went into its making. That deficiency marks many otherwise fine tomes. What we learn is **told** instead of **demonstrated**. We learn **what** was accomplished but not **how**. We are given a macrocosmic view of the company or venture, a view not allowing us to peer into the mysteries of what happens, into what people **actually do**. So, then, the idea for "Avatar."

The Series is pragmatic, intelligent, informed. The authors have been selected or selected the series because it offers the opportunity to spell out the processes of successful business enterprise on a **human scale**. In short, manifestations of governing or aggregate ideas in terms **of performance by individuals**. If there is more to learn and refine by such an approach, we are willing and, we hope, wise enough to incorporate such knowledge into as yet undreamed and unwritten titles in this Series.

Kenneth Friedenreich, Ph.D.
Series Editor

Preface

You probably enjoy prefaces just about as much as I do. So I'll be very brief.

Let me assure you of two things: first of all, you're going to enjoy reading this book. It might even be downright fun for you. Secondly, the magic sell works. The best thing about the magic sell is that these techniques and example scenarios work as soon as you use them. And then you just keep using them. Watching it all come together almost immediately does seem like a feat of magic—for you and your customer.
Stan Adler

STEP ONE
Setting the Stage
For the Magic Sell

Get a Headstart
With the Right Attitude

IF I ASKED YOU to tell me in one sentence or less what makes one CE salesperson more successful than another—what would you say? Take a moment and give it some thought. Some of you might answer, "Stan. He really knows the equipment." Others might say, "She knows how to make a good impression." A few of you might tell me, "He's really got his act together." And for others it might be, "She's successful because she knows how to get behind the product." And you would all be right because you're all talking about a single aspect of the same thing. I can sum up that single most important attribute in one word. *Attitude.* Your attitude towards selling will determine how well you sell. It's as simple as that—and as important as that. Each of your answers described an aspect of a salesperson with the right attitude.

So before I talk about how to start practicing the steps of the magic sell, let's discuss your attitude, which we'll assume is excellent, but... perhaps could still use a little improvement on occasion.

First, let me mention that there are a couple of words that bounce around the world of sales which are about as helpful as a hockey stick in a tennis match. Words like "strategy" and "tactics." You may have even heard people talking about "strategizing"—which, correct me if I'm wrong, is something you do when you get tired of trying to communicate. The potentially bad thing about words like these is that they imply that you are going to do something *to* the customer rather than *with* the customer. When I hear salespeople talk strategy and tactics, I usually think of things like ambush, plan of attack, defense and offense. I imagine General Patton studying a map of Sicily with one of the most worried looks of the 20th century. Exciting stuff . . . but not the kind of thing that makes for good selling.

Words like "strategy" and "tactics" are often part of the vocabulary and attitude of an undistinguished salesperson (undistinguished for a very good reason, which we'll get to). These words are control-oriented. Now obviously you have to be in control of the sale, but your customer had also better be in charge of his or her purchase. Control-oriented words can tend to build an attitude that is more dominating than cooperative. If you've been using these words, you probably found yourself consciously thinking more about doing something *to* someone rather than making something happen *with* someone. And that may be why you have not been as successful as some of the other salespeople in your store.

Selling, however, doesn't exist in a vacuum—as a world unto itself—so think about any personal relationship you might have had that was based on doing *to* rather than doing *with* and you'll probably come up with an experience you would just as soon forget. That's because successful relationships, whether personal or professional, are based on *mutual satisfaction*—two words that should be part of your vocabulary, and which you'll be hearing often . . . because mutual satisfaction is key to the magic sell.

But what about the seemingly successful salesperson whom we've all known who seems to have been raised on a steady diet of Clint Eastwood movies. He's the one-hit man. A label that would probably appeal to this type of salesperson until he realized what it really meant. The customer is asked to state his reason for being in the store. After looking the customer up and down with a devastating squint, the salesperson points first to the customer and then at a tape deck and says, "That's the deck for you." And when the customer actually buys it, the salesperson finds the purchase hard to explain. So does the customer. Because when he gets home and thinks about what happened, he's still not sure whether he made a good or bad choice. The customer must then rationalize the purchase as being a good one and pretend that he actively made it, because no one likes to admit he's been led by the nose and that he wasn't given the opportunity to really make a choice at all. Eventually, all he'll remember is being told to do something, like a child obeying a grown-up's command, and his new tape deck becomes a vivid reminder of a bad experience.

The customer won't be back. The one-hit man doesn't get a second chance. And isn't this also the reason why this salesperson is undistinguished compared to some of his peers? He's like so many other salespeople out there who can intimidate the customer into doing something once, without regard for the customer's needs. Good customers distinguish good salespeople, and the one-hit man doesn't have any. Ask him who's a good customer, and he'll answer, "Somebody with money in his pocket." He forgets that the person with money in his or her pocket knows other people who also carry around currency. And when he says, "Now don't forget to tell your friends about me," he doesn't realize what kind of impression he made and what kind of things the customer is going to tell his friends. He's going to have to wait for the next ad and an unsuspecting new customer before doing business again—all because of a warped selling attitude on the part of a salesperson whose goal should be controlling his *attitude* and not his *customer*. If you want to see the same customer more than once, you have to act like it, thus building your own reputation (which means sales) and that of the store.

Don't think of the customer as a competitor, as someone you must score on in order to feel good about yourself. You've got enough competitors in the consumer electronics market without creating more. In fact, all your customer wants is the same thing you want—cooperation. Your customer wants to buy every bit as much as you want to sell. And if you regard the customer as a potential friend, you can be assured that your attitude will be —in a word—friendly. Of course it's true that not all customers come in acting as if they want to make friends, and this is mainly because of something I've already mentioned—unpleasant experiences with dominating salespeople. They're wary, thus giving you a chance to make up for their attitude by treating them in a friendly, open manner.

How you act determines how others act. How you talk will determine how others talk. If one eyebrow is raised and your chin is lowered as if you were looking down the barrel of a carbine, the customer who just walked in to ask about CD players is now asking himself why he ever came to your place. If he hasn't turned around and exited by now, he's probably headed for the nearest rack system to hide behind while he regroups. Or how would the customer feel if you walked up to him and, out of the corner of your mouth, said, "So guy, what brought you in today?" He might feel as if he's being set up, or that he's being challenged. For certain, he feels as though he's being treated as a typical customer rather than as somebody special. He will seriously wonder how to get out of this uncomfortable situation—and once the customer's found the way out, he'll stay out.

I certainly hope you don't think these two examples are farfetched, because unfortunately I've witnessed this type of sales behavior by too many people on too many floors. Remember that the customer is somebody special, and somebody you don't take for granted. After everything is said and done, the customer is really the only person who can make you a success.

So even though the customer may not have come in with a face full of smiles and a fistful of dollars, he did come in to see *you*. He came at the invitation of your ads, or because of the OPEN sign on your door or because somebody recommended your store as the right place. And because you're doing what you're doing by choice—nobody said, "Be a CE salesperson *or else*!"—it's now up to you to perform the role of host. Not only is it your responsibility to be a good host, but it is decidedly to your advantage. Making the customer's first visit worthwhile will result in his visiting you again. And increased business is the headstart you're looking for.

You want to make sure that what you say and what you do will make both you and your customers feel good enough to make the purchase and, *in addition*, feel such a sense of satisfaction that they will tell other people about what a great time it was doing business with you. Word of mouth is the most powerful and sought after form of endorsement in this business, and it can work both for you and against you. Statistically, every customer who has a bad experience will tell twelve other people, and *thirteen percent of them will tell twenty others*. You've heard that bad news travels fast? That's how fast. But you won't have to worry about that ominous statistic if you're practicing the techniques exampled by each step of the magic sell. Instead, you will be able to turn that statistic around and use it to your advantage. If you're the first salesperson the customers meet when they start shopping for their new TV, they'll find a salesperson who is everything they wanted but quite possibly did not expect to find. It's your opportunity to take advantage of the status quo, and surprise the customer with your sincere regard for their needs, and to use your refined skills and show them how to make a satisfactory purchase. And if you're the third or fourth in line, you'll be amazed at how quickly you're able to turn their fears and frowns into satisfied smiles.

Every satisfied customer of yours will eventually tell a dozen other people, and a significant percentage of them will tell more people who will tell even more people. Good business doesn't stop as long as you keep making a concerted effort to do your best. You will have discovered the advantage that accrues to every successful sales professional: an established network of preferred customers to assure you of sales, regardless of ads that don't work, Sunday football, weather, or other factors that might otherwise inhibit business. And now the customers who come in to see you *will* be acting like friends—a good share of them will seem like old friends. You'll be in demand because of the goal which you've worked hard to attain—that of consistently creating positive and productive relationships between you and your customers.

The very fact that you started reading this book tells you that you're serious about your career as a CE salesperson. There are many people who have sold for years without realizing who they are, where they are, or how they think and act relative to their customers. Consequently, they never really excel at their profession. But you're different. You realize that you can always get better at what you do—and you will.

To Compete, Get To Know the Competition

COMPETITIVE. Over and over again, that's how people on the inside describe the consumer electronics industry. And the truth is that you *are* in one of the most competitive retail businesses of this decade. Thus, to succeed, you have to know your competition as well as you know your own store.

You've probably been told at one time or another that it's important to get to know the competition. And you may have agreed, but figured that it's something that will come with experience. That's like the football coach saying, "I'll know more about the Bears after we play them a few times." Guess how long he'll be coaching. And guess how long you'll be selling if you wait to learn about your competition. Nothing in the book of selling is just a matter of time; success in selling means planning. Selling is a well-thought-out action plan.

You should, in fact, get to know the competition before you get to know your customer. Why? Because there's always the chance that your customer didn't come to your store first. And finding out where the customer has shopped can be as important to you as knowing what the customer is shopping for. But knowing that your customer has been to XYZ Inc. before coming to you will not really do you any good unless you make it your business to know more than "a couple of things" about XYZ Inc.

New products and innovations are offered by over a thousand different manufacturers. These products are spread

out among a vast array of dealers, and the result can sometimes be a thoroughly confused consumer. After a while,
everything starts to look alike—the products, the store and the
ads. At that point, customers often do one thing, and that is to
actively search out one distinguishing factor—price. But price
is a short-lived reason for shopping at a particular store. Next
week the store across the street may advertise the lowest
price on a particular product, and guess where your customer
will go?

You are the only reason why the customer won't go
across the street for this week's "lowest" price. Customers
will continue to shop at your store if they feel they are getting
something more valuable than low price. The customer of the
eighties needs your expertise. This is one of the main reasons
that the business community regards sales training as essential
to today's retail business. It is you, the salesperson, that builds
a strong and loyal clientele. The marketing department has
discovered its limits. Giving away a bicycle with the purchase
of a new TV or free coupons redeemable at your local Rent-a-
Video store when you buy a VCR may be a reason to come to
your store for as long as the promotion lasts, but what happens after that? The customer will come back to the same
place if, and only if, he receives professional, personal service. Price and promotion is a reason for buying once, but it is
not the reason for buying twice at the same place.

But don't take my word for it. Think about how you
yourself shop. Do you frequent one gas station more than any
other? If you do it's probably not solely because of the price or
the octane rating of the gas. Maybe it's because of the attend-
ant who waived the deposit on the gas can when you ran out
of gas a year ago, and whom you now know on a first-name
basis. Maybe it's because of the person who reminded you of
the warranty on your battery and that it would be replaced
free of charge just when you were pulling out your credit
card. Or maybe it was the person who offered to pour a can of
oil for you even though you paid for self-service. The reason
for patronizing one gas station over another inevitably has
something to do with an aspect of service.

And if you owned a gas station, it would be to your
advantage to know that the station across the street didn't

charge deposits on gas cans in an emergency, that battery warranties were honored and that occasionally full-service privileges were extended to self-service customers. If you didn't upgrade your service standards to meet the competition, you would likely end up spending your days just watching the cars roll in and out of the other station, wondering what was so magical about the other side of the street.

The same holds true for electronics retailing. Knowing the competition—their strengths and weaknesses—helps you keep up. Better yet, it means that you get the edge. *Knowing the competition means that you can compete!* Ignoring the competition will leave you flat-footed and empty-handed. And merely following the competition could be like getting caught in the slipstream of an eighteen-wheeler that you hope is going the same place you are.

Suppose a customer has rattled through all of the newspaper ads, thumbed through the inserts, talked to friends, and finally decided to go out and do it. Since it's obviously not an impulse buy, it's unlikely that he or she will say, "First stop and I'll pop for it." It's unlikely—but it can happen. It depends on you, the salesperson. If you're prepared and you know the competition as well as you should, you can, in effect, do the shopping for the customer.

If you know what everyone else has to offer relative to what you can offer, and you present both sides with a sense of respect and credibility, you can save the customer the fatigue of shopping and allow the customer to make his or her purchase at the first stop. Even better, that customer will come back to you because you are knowledgeable, well-informed and concerned about helping the customer make the right purchase at the right place. Otherwise you wouldn't have gone to the trouble of explaining in detail the advantages and disadvantages of one place or brand over another. Because you've demonstrated that you know what you're talking about—that you know the competition on more than a superficial basis—you can talk with confidence about the advantages of buying from you and your company. You will not find yourself waging a one-man smear campaign against the competition. You'll be selling from an accurate and honest perspective based on research.

Getting to know the competition isn't difficult. It's a matter of taking the time to visit other stores and reading their ads. Your knowledge of the competition should include the answers to the following basic questions:

- How many consumer electronics stores or departments are within a convenient driving radius? (*Does their location have easy access or offer convenient parking?*)
- What products or services do they offer? (*Is their strength in variety, uniqueness, or depth of product? Do they offer self-service or home-delivery service?*)
- Do they offer exclusive brands, services, or plans which are superior to your own? (*What alternatives can you offer to counter these exclusives? Are the perceived advantages practical or a chrome-trim package?*)
- What does the inside of the store or department look like? (*Is it merchandising by design or stack-it-anywhere? Do you want to stay or do you get a sudden longing for fresh air? Do you feel closed in, lost, or perfectly comfortable? Do they have departments that define the product or confuse the customer?*)
- Do they have professional salespeople? (*Do they rely on can-I-help-you methods or do they know how to sell? Would you buy from them if you were in a different business?*)
- Do they offer service, warranty, or extended maintenance agreements? (*Do they have an easy exchange or refund policy? Do they scream service, or is it a known fact that they do well by their customers?*)

How the competition's advertising compares with your own deserves your special attention. Find out the following: *What form of media or print do they use? How often? What is the theme—service, price, exclusive or institutional? What ads do they run and when? Is it a clearance, the weekly 25%-Off sale, a once-a-year white-flower day, an after-Christmas 50%-off everything sale, a V.I.P. midnight event, a pre-CES or a post-CES sale, a fire sale, a going-out-of-business or a grand opening sale?*

The more you know in advance the better off you'll be.

Studying the competition's ads means you won't be caught humming if a customer suprises you by saying, "XYZ Inc. is selling their Walkman for a lot less." On the surface that might appear to be the case, but because you've studied their ad, you might know, for example, that their Walkman is not AM/FM and does not record. Your customer will be impressed and pleased that you saved him a useless trip, and he is quite likely to buy from you.

Of course, it is equally important to know your own store's ads. After all, they contain some of your most important lines. What does the customer expect to hear from you or expect you to show him? Know what products you are selling and for how long at what price. Your customers do not come to you for a history lesson—they want to know what you can offer them today and for how much and what's coming tomorrow and next year. . . . Getting tomorrow's product today is the great idea of the CE industry.

So how do you do your research? Do what a salesperson does best when he or she is not selling—shop. Take your time and have fun watching other people sell to you. And listen carefully to the media. Don't turn off the ads—it's part of the retail tradition. Find out what the store down the block is saying about itself. Compare its version of a good value to yours.

When you shop, go one step further. Look at the other salesperson and imagine how you would sell the same product—even if it's a different product from what you carry. How would you make the same scene better?

Avoid Losses By Always
Knowing Where You Are

IMAGINE THE LAST TIME you were talking to a customer, describing the benefits of one component over another. Recall how he seemed to be agreeing with everything you said, only then to walk out the door without buying anything. While such rejections inevitably confront all salespeople at one time or another, knowledgeable professionals can minimize them by knowing exactly where they are at any given moment in their workday.

Let me give you an example of what I mean by that. Suppose an air traffic controller asked a 747 pilot, "Where are you?" The pilot's answer should include such information as altitude, air speed, wind turbulence and direction as well as where he is and where he's going to be. In short, he would give a detailed professional appraisal of his present location. If you're a passenger on that plane you had better hope that your pilot's answer is a little more detailed than, "I'm up in the air," or you might be in for a bumpy ride.

If I ask, "Where are you?" and you answer, "I'm in the video department," your answer would technically be right, but not right enough to do you or your customer any good. You'd both be in for a bumpy ride because in order for the customer to enjoy his experience in your store, you'll have to "pilot" him in a professional manner. That means you have to know exactly where you are and where you're going.

At first glance, comparing your job to an airline pilot's

may seem farfetched. But passengers and customers do have similar concerns. They want to make sure their trip is comfortable and enjoyable. They want first-class treatment regardless of the price of the ticket or the system. They must feel secure if the unexpected should occur, such as turbulence or a change of price or a misadvertised product. They must have confidence in you and your ability. They're looking for signs of credibility and they want reassurance that they have come to the right place. If the trip or purchase is taking more or less time than expected, they want to know why. They're looking for peace of mind not the thrill of a lifetime. And if their trips are comfortable, and they feel their time, energy and money have been spent wisely, they will do business with you again. And you will have made for a profitable and personally-rewarding CE sales career.

Now if I were to ask, "Where are you?" you can give me your own detailed professional appraisal of your present position: "I'm at the front counter, a couple of minutes past opening the store. I've already checked out the day's advertisements of both my store and of my competitors' stores, and I've taken a quick inventory of what equipment I have both on display and in the stockroom. I've straightened up a couple of loose hanging power cords that were looking sloppy. I've got a pen handy and I'm ready to greet the first customer of the day."

Does this resemble your own routine each morning prior to opening? If not, it should. Regardless of whether you're a salesperson, a pilot, a lawyer or movie director, all successful professionals practice the same five P's—*Proper Planning Prevents Poor Performance.*

Now let's study how to put that rule into practice. In the last chapter we talked about how important it is to know your competition and how they do business, and that you should be buying a morning paper each day and studying both the competition's ads as well as your own. Remember, studying these ads on a daily basis is your only opportunity to prepare your sales plan in advance.

The other essential reading material for CE salespeople that shouldn't be overlooked is magazines. Consumer electronics "buff books" such as *Audio* (especially the October

Annual Equipment Directory), *Stereo Review, Video Review,* and several others will keep you updated on the new equipment that your customers will be asking you about. As a professional CE salesperson you need to keep abreast of any new innovations in the consumer electronics market. Unless you know more about the latest equipment than the customer does, you are going to find it very difficult, nearly impossible, to exhibit the expertise which he expects. And just because you may not stock a particular product or brand of equipment is no reason to ignore it. Your customer has not confined his or her awareness to only those products which your store carries. Being knowledgeable even about equipment you don't carry proves to your customer that you really know your field and not just what's on your shelves. That instills trust, which obviously makes for better sales since the customer will be on your side.

You will be getting only part of the story, however, if you only read the consumer magazines. Equally important as a source of information are the trade magazines, such as *Audio Times*. These magazines are not readily available to the consumer, and thus are written specifically for you, the professionals of the consumer electronics business. They are your opportunity to familiarize yourself with the marketing and operational aspects of the business as well as finding advance information and behind-the-scenes material on the latest products.

To get the most out of any magazine, trade or consumer, you should be reading not only the new product write-ups and feature articles, but also the advertisements as well. And pay particularly close attention to the ad copy. If a manufacturer and its advertising agency consider the copy convincing enough to sell the product to you, you should certainly be using it to sell the product to your customer. Try using this line the next time you're demonstrating a set of speakers: "They have clean, crisp highs and deep, rich bass." Manufacturers have used variations of this phrase for years. Try one yourself, and don't be surprised if customers nod their heads and say, "That's exactly what I'm looking for."

Meanwhile, take note of other things that you must be aware of before opening your doors. A quick inventory check at the start of each day will prevent embarrassments later on. Suppose you were to spend half an hour extolling the features and benefits of one model VCR over another, only to find that you don't have it in stock. There is very little chance of saving the sale after that occurs. Also familiarize yourself with where your advertised items are located on the floor. If a customer comes in to see the new monitor that you have advertised and you cannot lead him directly to it, you have lost his confidence before you even start. How would you like to get on the plane and hear your pilot saying, "Albuquerque . . . Albuquerque . . . now let's see, I knew where that was yesterday."

How important is having a pen handy? Extremely important. I've seen more than one sale lost when a salesperson has had to abandon the customer to search for a pen.

Once the salesperson has left, so goes his opportunity to make the sale, as the customer begins second-guessing the purchase, and ends up going home to think it over. (By the way, invest five dollars or more on the pen and you'll be less apt to leave it somewhere and lose it. This small investment will pay for itself many times over in the course of your career.)

Being prepared also means making sure that all product sheets, literature, and all forms required to make the sale are in the proper place and are in plentiful supply. The last thing you want to do after establishing verbal agreement is to scurry around looking for a piece of paper to finalize the sale.

You must also make it your personal responsibility to maintain a supply of records, tapes, or CD's that represent a variety of tastes. You never want to demonstrate an audio system using a worn-out, scratchy record or a VCR with a tape that has glitches and dropouts galore. The quality of the software determines the quality of the sound or picture, and the customer can listen to scratchy records and watch blurry images at home.

How neat is your store? Are the power cords nice and straight? Are the televisions all properly tuned? Is everything clean? In short, does your store project a professional image? These are the things which the customer will notice immediately. It will only take a few minutes of your time to keep things in order if you keep up with them every day. If it's not your job, *make* it your job—or make sure someone gets it done. Remember, just as you are a reflection of the store, the store is a reflection of you.

That brings us to you. Do you look, act, and sound like the professional you want to be? Successful CE salespeople constantly work on their grooming, manner, and delivery. There is a familiar saying about the importance of first impressions which we will be discussing in an upcoming chapter, and I'll share with you then the steps that you need to make an honest assessment of yourself.

Now that you have reviewed what you should be doing prior to opening your doors for the day's business, your day will undoubtedly run much smoother. You are prepared, and that can't help but inspire confidence among your customers. Now if I ask you in the middle of the afternoon, "Where are you?" you can answer, "Stan, I'm a couple minutes past the sale of a $400.00 VCR, and a few steps away from greeting that customer who's scouting that monitor. Before that, I'm going to say goodbye to my VCR customers and encourage them to enjoy their new purchase."

You will be able to answer this way because you have developed a keener sense of where you are and where you are going. In filing a detailed "flight plan" with yourself, you now project a poised, professional presence that inspires confidence in your customer. That means easier sales, satisfied customers and more money in your pocket at the end of the month. Remember, whether you're a pilot in the air or a salesperson on the floor, it's critical to always know where you are at all times.

STEP TWO
The Attitude You Forgot
That Still Works

The Attitude You Forgot
That Still Works

SAY, "HI." Say it again—out loud this time. It's not much of a word at all, is it? If someone asked you what it meant you'd probably pause and say something like, "It's just something you say when you see someone." But that doesn't really define the word, does it? That definition doesn't do the word justice. It doesn't take into account how important the word can be.

When you say something like "Hi" or "Hello" you usually expect a similar response. If you don't get it, you feel embarrassed, ignored or conspicuous—as if everybody else saw the other person fail to respond to your greeting. As simple as the greeting may be, it can sometimes be very difficult to say. Remember when you were a teenager? Almost all of us at one time or another experienced difficulty in saying "Hi" to the right person at the right time. "Go ahead, just say 'Hi,' she's not going to bite you," or "Say 'Hi' to him, he's just a person," are things your friends or parents probably said. But to you, he or she wasn't *just* a person. And though it might have taken you some tossing and turning in your sleep and a week of rehearsing in front of the mirror, when you finally got up the courage to say it, one of two things happened. The person said "Hi" and possibly smiled awaiting your next words (which thankfully were faster in coming than the first one) or the person acted as if he or she didn't hear you. How you felt after either one of these two scenarios is still pretty easy to remember isn't it?

If the person responded positively, you probably didn't think about much of anything else for the rest of the day. The "Hi" in combination with the smile played repeatedly in your mind and you felt great, maybe even slightly heady, every time you thought about it. That first short, sweet plunge into an interpersonal relationship with a person whom you didn't really know very well but wanted to know better was exciting and fun. But what about the other time? You said "Hi" and he or she just kept fiddling with their locker combination as if you weren't even there. You probably didn't even bother to say "Hi" a second time. One more rejection like that could have you doubting your own existence. Your self-esteem was hanging by a shoestring. So to get yourself back together, you probably found a friend as quickly as possible and started talking about what a jerk the person of your dreams turned out to be.

"Hi" just barely qualifies as a word, but the dynamics of what can happen after that single syllable is uttered, has been the basis for countless novels, plays, movies, songs and TV shows. Your greeting in the CE store can be equally vitalizing or devastating. It can mean the difference between being a mediocre salesperson (that's the person who is just doing what he's doing until the movie contract comes through) or a top-performing CE sales professional (and that can be you).

A 1983 survey of top selling CE salespeople revealed that the most difficult area of sales technique was, by a wide margin, opening up the sale. These sales superstars felt that once the initial contact was made, everything else—relatively speaking —was easy. So even though you're past high school, the word "Hi" or an equivalent greeting still plays an important part in your life. Now it's your livelihood, instead of a date, that depends on your effective use of the word.

Sometimes, with even the best of you, circumstances will hinder your ability to say "Hi" effectively. Maybe your alarm clock doesn't go off and you end up with a speeding ticket trying to make it to work on time. Your manager comes down hard on your case for being two minutes late, and in the same breath docks your sales incentives for the day and tells you to "go over there and take care of those customers!" If you go over to the customers in a foul mood and they pick up on it, or, even worse, if you take your hostility out on them, you can be sure of one thing. You're wasting your time because you're not going to be selling anything. "But Stan," you say, "what do you think I am? How could I *not* be in a rotten mood? I'm not superhuman, I've got emotions!" Of course you do, but you've got to check your negative ones at the door. Good salespeople are a lot like actors. An actor probably has the best display of emotions of anyone you can think of, but an actor upon taking the stage can't say, "Bring the curtain back down and we'll start over again later. I'm in a bad mood right now." And you can't either.

Quickly dismissing a bad mood isn't something that's foreign to your nature. In fact, when you were a lot younger you used to do it all the time. You too were a charter member of the terrible two's. There you'd be, your tiny fists all clenched up, your shiny face rapidly turning from a crimson hue to a full-fledged beet red, the water works were ready to spring and a wail that would rival a rapidly approaching banshee was all set to start. For reasons beyond anybody's comprehension you were in the clutches of a major TT (temper tantrum). But suddenly you spied a butterfly and the crisis was over. You were smiling and giggling and chasing that butterfly as if it were the most wonderful thing in the world. And whatever was causing your previous discomfort was lost in the wind.

When you were no longer upset, you didn't feel guilty, or blame someone for getting you mad, or fear repercussions for your previous behavior. Instead, you were content to be yourself. You were ready to be nice again.

Now I'm not saying that you should revert to infantile standards of behavior and indulge in rapid and extreme mood swings. I'm saying that you need to recapture the ability that you had as a child to focus all your attention on one moment at a time. Successful salespeople are able to concentrate and maintain a positive focus on a given situation. As far as they're concerned, nothing has happened prior to that moment in their day and nothing is in the future except their next customer. There are no negative thoughts about punitive managers or rude customers. They know, and so do you, that those thoughts aren't going to help make the next sale. And their ability to maintain their positive focus isn't some mysterious process either. It's a matter of being nice. That's right, being nice.

Now I realize that you can't just go out and be nice because somebody tells you to, any more than you can go out and fall in love because somebody told you to. You have to feel like being nice. You have to be sincere or you'll look like the patented American stereotype of the "salesman." You know the type, the 70mm gum-to-gum grinner with a how-ya-doing-today, glad-to-meetcha, guess-what-I'm-gonna-do-for-you spiel. Those are the people who parody the profession you practice.

In the early sixties, I had the pleasure to talk at some length with a Chicago bluesman, and I will never forget a phrase that he used which he found especially significant. "It's nice to be nice," he said with a smile, pausing, and then, more seriously, he repeated it to me as if it were a secret message —"It's *nice* to be nice." I repeated the phrase for years without knowing what it really meant. It was a phrase that I had to grow into. To talk about the full significance of the phrase would take too long, but look at it this way: to just "be nice" is to do something for the sake of doing it, but "to be nice" because "it's nice to be nice" is something else entirely. It's doing something because you feel it.

When was the last time you were living proof of that phrase? Let me help you out. Remember the Saturday when you had sold 3K in key 1 by noon, and somebody walked in holding up a headshell with a cartridge but no stylus? He had a look on his face as if he were ready to confess or cry or both, and without waiting for him to say a word, you gently reached out and, taking the headshell from his hand, said, "Looks like you might have a little problem here. Hold on, I'll be right back." After finding a suitable stylus replacement, you brought it back to him and placed it in his palm, saying, "There. Nothing to it." When he asked how much he owed you, you replied, "It's on the house. You might need a new turntable someday, and I'd appreciate your looking me up." The customer in need found a salesperson he will never forget, and he's experienced one of those rare shopping experiences which he can't wait to tell somebody about. It's *nice* to be nice.

What do you think inspired you to do something that another person won't soon forget and is still telling other people about? What is the secret to being nice and feeling good about feeling that way? It's pretty simple, isn't it? When you're doing good business, you feel good about yourself, and other people too. But when you're hammered by the clock you don't feel that you have time to be nice. You look at every customer as a chance to make up for the one you just lost. And as a result, you just keep losing them. The reason they keep walking away empty-handed is because you've become desperate and you're pressing too hard. You're no longer being yourself. Understandably, you are trying to make up for all the things that went wrong, but the smile on your face is no match for the dollar signs in your eyes. You are looking for a customer to get you out of a hole that he's had nothing to do with.

Though I mentioned the clock, time really has nothing to do with the situation we're talking about—generally called a slump. Time is always on your side if you have the right viewpoint, and feel good about what you're doing. Whether you're relaxing or working, time is really not something you pay much attention to if you're using each minute in a productive way, and making positive moves all the way. "Time flies when you're having fun." Sure it's trite, but it sure is true. Time tends to be of little concern when you're concentrating on something that you enjoy doing, and are absorbed in doing it as well as you possibly can.

Chances are that when you sold that three grand in three hours or less, it wasn't just to one person. There were probably a stack of invoices that included everything from patch cords to big screen TV's. And when the customer with the missing stylus came in and you happened to glance at your watch, you were probably amazed that the day was almost half-gone. When you are involved, and have got your whole self into your job, you tend to make the right moves and have a sense of timing and grace that has everybody in the store marveling. . . . Everybody but you—because you don't have time for mirrors when you're really relating to somebody else.

When you have this wonderful momentum, you are being yourself completely—you don't have time for personas, affectations, or crazy moves that may entertain you and a few other salespeople. Greeting a customer with, "How you doin' man, Billy Wonkers, commando of audio-video, servant of sight-and-sound at your service!" is a cool greeting that will get a cool reception and confirm every *bad* thing that the customer has ever heard about the CE business. Instead, how about this? "Hi. Welcome to AVC." You'll probably get a smile and a "thank you" in the first few seconds of meeting the customer, rather than raised eyebrows or an embarrassed giggle.

Treating yourself and your customers as if you've had a 3K morning every day doesn't take an act of magic, but it does mean mastering each of the seven steps of the magic sell so that everything flows without your having to consciously think about each technique as you use it. Mastering the magic sell simply means practicing it—starting with friends, members of your family, and your very next customer.

Super CE salespeople follow the steps of the magic sell as a matter of course. And super CE salespeople are nice people. Recently I was talking to a friend, whom I feel to be an astute observer of sales technique, about a CE superstar who was close to the six-million-dollar mark. I asked what he felt made this person so successful. After giving it some thought, he said, "He's just a real nice guy. He does everything that we've always talked about, follows up on all of his customers, always shows up ready to sell. But the truth of the matter is that he's is just a really nice guy. I wish I could do better than that Stan, but that's all I can really put my finger on."

My friend had no reason to feel perplexed, because he had identified one of the most important characteristics of a top performer. And, of course, it makes perfect sense when you think about it. Refined sales technique has never been a matter of a trick move, contrivance, clever line or trap-door close. . . . It's finally a matter of being yourself as superbly as you have ever imagined yourself, and never losing your concentration while you're in a sales situation. When you're good and you know it, you feel good—and when you feel good, you feel like being nice.

But what if you're in a slump, and it feels as though someone just stole all your timing and finesse? That's an important question, and I could answer it by discussing burn-out and how to counter it as if it were a problem as difficult to overcome as the common cold. Or I could suggest listening to inspirational and motivational tapes, and have you jogging to *Chariots of Fire* or doing aerobics to the beat of *Flashdance*. Or we might talk about standing in front of the mirror and enunciating tongue-twisters with a million-dollar smile, or doing mental push-ups, or checking out your daily priorities versus your lifetime goals, because goal-setting is an important part of any salesperson's life. Or we could talk about a lot of other things that can work to pull you out of the dumps and out of your slumps, but right now, slip away from your slump just long enough to read the rest of this book—and then take an approach to selling that will have you making sales rather than thinking about them.

Most slumps occur because the salesperson decided to *let* it happen instead of *making* it happen, so the customers stopped buying when the salesperson stopped selling. There is only one real solution to a slump . . . making a sale. And that's why the magic-sell approach is a solution. It works. When you try it for the first time and it works, you'll feel good. When it works the second time, you'll feel even better. And very soon, you'll feel very good about being good. It's a nice feeling you won't keep to yourself. Other people can't help but pick up on it. Take my word for it—it's nice to be nice.

So if you're waiting to sell three grand by noon before you feel right enough to treat your customers in a special way, then you're missing a lot of opportunities to generate loyal customers. When you're practicing the philosophy of "It's nice to be nice," it doesn't take money to motivate your day— but more money is what you'll end up with, since you'll be a better and more accommodating salesperson. You may find yourself motivated by the quality of a certain kind of sale, or because you turned a frustrated and embittered shopper into a satisfied and trusting customer. I'm sure you've met the guy who walks in with a frown on his face and a newspaper insert rolled up in his fist. Before you can even say "Hi" he says, "Do you guys have any of this stuff in stock or is it just another one of your come-on's?"

Rather than blaming the customer or classifying his abrasive intro as unreasonable and unworthy of your attention, take the right perspective. Make the effort to empathize. How would you feel if you had just made a special trip to a store that advertised a substantial discount on an item, only to find out that you had wasted your time and two dollar's-worth of gas because the item was not in stock? So of course he has a right to be annoyed, but that doesn't give him the right to pull you down to his mood. Remind yourself that you are a CE salesperson by choice, and that this customer and his problem is as much a part of your job as the smiling person who just bought a VCR. It's time to be professional. Be nice. Present yourself credibly and nine times out of ten you'll make that unhappy, suspicious customer happy because you understand how he feels.

Look at him and dare to smile. Apologize for the entire industry, and then tell him that buying something that is designed to bring pleasure into your life should be a pleasure to buy. Then offer to do something that will make up for all of his trouble—maybe this is the time to throw a record cleaner into the sale even before the customer chooses the component. And when he makes his purchase, he's going to leave your store feeling like telling the whole wide world that at last he's a satisfied customer. And you'll feel pretty satisfied, too.

Or maybe you feel too good to be true because the kid who has been paying you visits every day for the past two months—the same kid the other salespeople are calling 'your son' by now —suddenly shows up with his real father in tow. The father wants to thank you for the special attention you have shown his son, and would like to buy a quality audio system, something that will last and eventually accommodate video, for his graduation present. The father's pleased, the son's thanking you again and telling his father how he couldn't have done it without you, and you're pretty pleased that you didn't ignore the kid after the third or fourth time he came in to see you. "It's nice to be nice" pays off in rewards that are sometimes even greater than money, doesn't it?

So remember, feel good. You've chosen a challenging and rewarding career. Don't be thinking of yesterday's refund or last night's squabbles as you walk over to greet the new customer. The present and future consists solely of the customer walking through that door right now. Take a deep breath, smile, and say, "Hi."

Make A First Impression
Worth Remembering

"YOU NEVER GET a second chance to make a good first impression." You've probably heard that phrase before. But regardless of how often you've heard it, and how true it may be, it's startling how regularly it's forgotten.

Think about the automobile salesperson who walks up to you chewing gum and twirling a key at the end of his retractable key chain. Without a word from you, he starts telling you about the turbo-exchange evacuator which may well be the technological breakthrough of the decade and which happens to be under the hood of that dynamite little car which you just happen to be standing beside. Not surprisingly, you quickly become confused trying to figure out what he's saying, focus on his face, and avoid the twirling key all at the same time. So you tell him you're just killing time, and go in search of another dealership even though it means going out of town.

Or what about the salesperson in the chic new clothing store who approaches you and appears to be wearing at least three different outfits, all of which clash? She may get a discount on clothes, but you wonder why she has to wear all of them at the same time. Her apparel might be perfect for certain customers, but you feel pretty safe in assuming that that doesn't represent the biggest part of her clientele. Her personal taste has just discouraged a potential customer.

Both the auto salesperson and the clothing-store salesperson are more concerned with themselves than with you.

They look as though they want to look and talk about what *they* want to talk about because they're mostly concerned about making an impression, rather than a good first impression. Making an impression isn't difficult, but making a good first impression is a matter of care, skill, and development.

Albert Mehrabian and other famous communications experts have determined that fifty-five percent of initial communication is based on appearance. The other forty-five percent is based on what we say and how we say it. Obviously then, a good first impression is important because without it you are communicating with less than half your assets. Without saying a word, you may be sending your customer a half-good/half-bad message which could lose you the sale before you start.

Making a good first impression means that you don't have to spend valuable time compensating for what you forgot to do in the first place. How you look and act within the first few moments of the sale determines whether you succeed in creating that very special customer-salesperson relationship which is unique in retail—and the exclusive of the CE salesperson. It's the magic sell. And it makes your job as a CE salesperson exciting and remarkably effective.

Take a few moments and think about your selling environment. The products in your store may seem fairly routine to you, but to the customers they form an exciting backdrop of visual images and musical sounds. The customers find themselves surrounded by more new ideas and intriguing innovations per square foot than they ever thought possible. They're looking forward to buying things which they will use for their personal relaxation and entertainment, not something they need for purely practical reasons. In some cases they're looking to you and asking for your approval—"Tell me that it's alright to buy something which serves no real practical purpose other than my personal enjoyment and pleasure." They're not buying a washing machine because the old one broke. Even if they're buying a new television to replace the old one, they are excited! They get to think about stereo television! Remote control! Big picture! Clear, vivid images that come right off the screen! They can turn a room of their house into a theater—the audio/video room! The automatic timer on the new washing machine doesn't quite have the same appeal, or inspire the same kind of excitement.

And when people get excited about something that will provide them with personal pleasure and excitement, they want somebody to share their excitement. They want somebody to come to their party—which is one of the main reasons you find people bringing friends with them when they make their purchase. They may call the friend an expert—and he or she may well be—but the friend was actually invited to a celebration which you have the opportunity to host.

Your opportunity to host the celebration depends upon your making that good first impression. Most customers just don't have the time to get to know you, and you don't have the time to get to know them in any traditional sense. Instead, you can create the illusion of "more enjoyment than is possible in a specified timeframe"—which is the main feature of every electronic toy that you sell. They are designed, remember, to help us relax, to help us get away from it all. Twenty minutes with an A/V system between you and the customer and you can attain a degree of intimacy that would normally take days or years in the normal course of events. You learn his dreams, disappointments, plans for the future, his likes and dislikes, favorite movie or record, or the group that really made a difference in his life. And it's all a function of you and the music and the images—and your familiarity with the products you sell. The turntables, receivers, tape decks, CD players, speakers, VCR's, TV's and monitors are there to deliver the perfect illusion. But selecting the right product can seem risky and confusing if you are not there to validate the customer's decision to buy something. By taking the mystery out of the situation and putting the magic in, you become someone special with a special understanding of your customer's needs and expectations.

But it all has to start happening from the first moment they see you if it's going to happen at all. They are not going to say, "Well, I can't stand the guy's looks but I'll talk to him anyway." They want you to be the right salesperson from the start. They want their buying experience to be enjoyable and they want to get along with you. So let's examine what you need to know in order to get a good start, and make that good first impression.

How you dress is the aspect of appearance that dominates your customer's first impression of you. Your clothing and how you wear it is a legitimate concern of the customer. "But I dress the way I feel best," you may say. That may not, however, be in your best interest—if you're interested in selling for profit as well as fun. You may feel better in jeans and running shoes, and you may feel even better in a T-shirt and shorts—personally, those are options belonging strictly to you. But professionally, you dress to please more than one person. You dress to please the customer as well as yourself. As a CE salesperson, a three-piece suit is generally about as out of place as your favorite pair of faded blue jeans. The customer is looking for a credible appearance. Depending on your taste, that may mean chinos, a sweater and laundered shirt; a blazer, oxford shirt, and a pair of slacks; or a neat sport shirt and corduroys. For women, the equivalent type of dress is appropriate.

Whatever dress option you choose should present you in a light that doesn't distract from your products or clash with the environment in which you sell. Your customer shouldn't have to justify your appearance before dealing with the mysteries of the equipment. The standards of dress in our industry are less strict than in others, but that doesn't mean you should take advantage of the situation. As a rule of thumb, how you dress should make your average customer feel comfortable and confident in your ability, rather than slightly uncomfortable and suspicious of your ability.

After clothing, what we look like is the second most important aspect of our appearance. "Listen, I'm not going to change my looks even for a four-thousand dollar A/V system," you may say. And I'm certainly not suggesting that you get a face lift, tummy tuck, make-up kit or a pair of contact lenses. You know as well as I do that your customer isn't interested in what color your eyes are, but *is* interested in your level of interest, awareness, excitement and energy. And your eyes tell it all. Getting the amount of sleep that keeps you looking fresh isn't something you can afford to overlook. You want to look like a "nice," "friendly," "sincere," "honest," "sensible," "likable," or "pleasant" kind of person. The expression on your face will answer your customer's concern in the most positive kind of way if you are aware that how you look is really up to you and not a matter of genetics.

A smile, a relaxed expression, a concerned nod of your head, eyes wide with expectation—these are movements that are choreographed in patterns that are yours exclusively and work for you in ways that won't for someone else. You can greet a person very nicely by simply smiling, and without a word, let the customer know that you are the right salesperson.

Movements—how you approach the customer—whether you choose to shake hands, how you stand, are all decisions you need to make when meeting the customer. Jumping off the counter and into the arms of the customer is an exciting movement but it's hardly in keeping with their expectations. Strutting up and sticking out your hand like *shake it or else* is equally disconcerting. And running from the back of the store with a box in your hands and tagging the customer with a *"be right with you!"* as you pass by may suggest excitement and a high energy environment, but the customer is not going to feel as if he or she is going to get thoughtful and professional service. One way to find out the best way to approach your customer is to take a good reading of how the customer moves. The customer's movements will tell you whether he or she is in a hurry to do business, wants to make contact and then browse, or is confused and needs help. Remember . . . the point is to recognize and be recognized. How the customer dresses, what he looks like, what's in his eyes, how he talks and how he moves is all the information you need to put together an appropriate good first impression for each individual customer.

Now that you know the strategy involved in making a good first impression, it's important to remember to tailor your presentation to the customer's individual taste as well. Since most of what you sell has something to do with music and video, you should be aware of what is current and what is a classic in music, movies and video. (Becoming an aficionado in these fields should not be a chore; if it is, you're in the wrong business.) Branch out in your tastes. Rather than being content as the resident expert in sixties rock or science fiction movies, also learn about classical music and MGM musicals. Be ready to respect your customer's individual taste. There's no reason that the customer should have to listen to an early Jeff Beck jam session when he would prefer to listen to Vivaldi on that pair of speakers which he might buy if he likes what he hears.

The latest video by Huey Lewis might be a better choice for thirty televisions in synch than the latest effort by Twisted Sister. That's not to say that you can't have just as much fun in trying to come as close as possible to the desired request of a metal devotee. Coming as close as possible to your customer's taste is important. But since you usually don't have two thousand records and videos at your fingertips, you should look for records that cross-over. The latest Stevie Wonder may fill the bill for someone who likes ballads or "soul" or "funk," and Willie Nelson's *Stardust* may work for the person who likes "country" or for another person who prefers "easy listening." The only way you can get close to another person's taste in music and video is by personally developing a wide range of tastes. That means doing a lot of good listening and watching. Ignorance is not bliss in the CE store. And when you're looking to affect that bond between you, your customer and the product, you have to be playing the right tune. Who knows, even Lawrence Welk might blow a mean squeeze box once in a while.

Unfortunately, customers leave more often than they stay based on what they hear or see playing in the CE store. The fact that the magic sell happens less often than it could, should be incentive enough for you to start doing everything you can for those customers who have been disappointed too many times and are looking for the right salesperson with the right taste to come along. Watching a suspicious glare turn into an excited smile is an experience worth working for.

After you have made the magic sell, people will often ask you, "Haven't we met somewhere before?" or "Didn't you used to work at . . . ?" Having known you somewhere before is the only way that the customer can rationalize his positive and spontaneous feelings about you. He's amazed by the sense of closeness which he feesl toward you. He's depended upon your taste and good judgment, and has essentially turned over the decision-making process to you. The "practical concerns" which he came in ready to protect became your responsibility. He may have shared his secret ambitions, disappointments and expectations. He has talked with you in a spirit of confidentiality that's normally extended only to his best friends. He's gotten caught up in the excitement of you and your products, the magic devices that set the stage for the magic sell.

When you put it all together—your movements, manners, looks, concern and expertise—you will achieve the presence of a professional. And no matter how many salespeople and customers there are in the store, you won't need a name badge or a uniform to be recognized as the right salesperson.

STEP THREE
Finding the Buyer Behind the Person

Greet the Customer
Who Is Not "Just Looking"

What Does Talking Have to Do with Selling?

SO FAR, I'VE TALKED primarily about the physical and mental preparation necessary for a day's or a career's worth of selling. I've stressed the importance of a good attitude for both yourself and your customer, and talked about the importance of being nice. I've talked about the necessity of knowing your competition, and reviewed those things which you must do on a daily basis to properly prepare yourself for a good day in the the CE store. I've talked about first impressions, and how the complete sales approach can be derailed if the first impression is not a good one. And I've talked about how much the first word tells your customer about your ability to handle his situation, and how that word can either inspire confidence or confusion resulting in a satisfied customer who feels good about coming back again or a disgruntled shopper who won't be back.

And I suppose there is a possibility that some of you may have been thinking, "Okay, okay—that's great, but let's get to the selling part!" Well, that's a pretty normal reaction because for most people if you want to talk about selling, you usually talk about talking.

It is also how too much selling is done. It's been my observation that for a wide majority of salespeople, talking seems to be their only interest. It's almost as if there were this little neon sign blinking on and off in their minds, asking, "Have I said enough yet to make the sale?" And when their customers are talking, it's all too easy to tell that they're not listening. They're already preparing what they're going to say the second the customer stops talking. And when the salesperson finishes a sentence, the sign flashes on again, "Have I said enough yet?"

I'm going to ask you to discard that question as useless and replace it with one that's worthy of your attention. Ask yourself: "Have I said too much for the sale to happen?" That's right—too much. Because by talking too much, you often talk yourself right out of a sale. Before saying anything, you want to ask yourself if what you're about to say is worth your time or the customer's time.

What we've talked about so far has little to do with talking, but a lot to do with communicating...the kind of communication that accounts for over ninety percent of our communications with any person on any day, work or play, rain or shine. Remember, the communication experts calculate that what we look like comprises fifty-five percent of communication, and the other forty-five percent is broken down as follows: thirty-eight percent is how we say things and the other seven percent is the words we use. So what we've been discussing up to this point is the kind of communication that counts the most. Ironically, most of the books written about selling that reinforce traditional trends in "salesmanship" dedicate about ninety percent of the content to talking. But if only seven percent of your communication is a matter of words, it is a seven percent that can make you great or second-rate. Being second-rate does not mean that you are going to be unemployed, but this is not a book about how to keep your job. *The Magic Sell* is about how to *excell* at your job. So I would like you to mentally review what you've already read, or reread it, before reading another word. I make this request because I assume that you're reading *The Magic Sell* because you're seriously intent upon making the magic sell happen, and it cannot be done—*I repeat*—cannot be done, without a sincere commitment to the attitude, values, and preparation which the previous chapters have addressed.

Rather than asking yourself whether you have said enough to make the sale—which is the most common checkpoint—I suggested that you ask yourself whether you have said too much for the sale to happen. A good place to start asking yourself this question is right before greeting the customer. Before you say anything. The reason is because you have a natural tendency to say more than you need to— starting with the very first word. If all you do is say, "Hi" or "Hello" with a smile, and wait for a response, you have just used a technique which is used by less than two-percent of CE salespeople. The other ninety-eight percent will say something like, "Hi, how you doing today?" or, worse, "May I help you?" (All it takes is a quick visit to one of your competitors to quickly confirm this statistic.)

Let's follow through with both of the above greetings.

S (salesperson): Hi, how you doing today?

C (customer): Fine. Just looking right now thank you.

S: May I help you?

C: No thanks, I'm just looking.

What happened? Nothing. You greeted the customer and the customer said, "Go away, come back later." It wasn't as bad as being rejected by the person of your dreams when he or she paid more attention to a school locker than to you, but rejection is rejection, and it's never pleasant. You're not on the sales floor to be ignored or rejected, and especially not with your very first word. If this happened in a non-working situation, you would probably end up telling someone about this rude encounter. . . . "All I did was go up to this person and say 'Hi' and he had the nerve to say 'See you later'—like *get lost*, you know. A real jerk." If this same non-communication happened consistently, you would probably begin to think of yourself as some kind of social outcast.

As a CE salesperson you must be an expert communicator—which is not the same as an expert talker—if you're going to be an expert salesperson. The previous mini-scenarios clearly illustrate why. How can you possibly expect to feel good about yourself or your customer if you get ignored half of your working day? And how will you care enough about a job like that to adequately prepare for it? And why should you care about making a good first impression if half the people you greet say "Come back some other time." As far as being nice because you feel like being nice, well I suppose that could become a sore spot.

Are You Looking for Rejection or Mutual Satisfaction?

It's difficult, in fact, nearly impossible to do a good job selling if you spend half your time worrying about being ignored or rejected. Rejection is an aspect of selling, just as it is an aspect of life—but so many mediocre, and therefore frustrated, sales-people have told new salespeople about rejection (because they've had to tell someone) that it has become some sort of perverse ground-rule that you had better be prepared for loads of rejection if you're going into sales. Similarly, parents can tell their children that they had better be prepared for rejection if they are going to grow up and be adults—and parents do tell their children just that. But they then go on to teach them ways of getting along with their fellow humans that will minimize this brand of trauma.

Rejection may be a fact of life, but it's certainly not a theme or anthem to live by. And this applies to sales: you should guard against CE folklore, and be cautious in accepting supposed facts-of-the-floor if you want to set any personal records. If someone told you that the closing rate of the average CE store was twenty-eight percent, and even if it were true, I doubt if you would accept that as your goal if you were working to make a decent income.

And it's true that you do meet your share of people who say, "Just looking," or, "I'll think it over," before saying, "I'll take it." That just means you should go one step further and find a way to greet the customer in a way that will have the customer telling you his or her needs rather than mouthing an automatic response which he or she dislikes saying as much as you dislike hearing it. "Just looking" is the cliche that more than any two words in sales says *mutual dissatisfaction*. So let's greet the customer in a way that will allow you to do your job better and in a way that will have you enjoying what you're doing even more. Selling is just like dancing, swimming, singing, or anything else in life—the better you get at it, the more you enjoy it.

As the customer approaches you or as you approach the customer, think only of the customer. Forget about the customer who just phoned with a service problem or the big credit ap that may clear this afternoon. Maybe selling is more like dancing than you thought. When you're dancing with someone and want to look good, you've got to concentrate on the other person's movements . . . not on the person across the floor or on the leader of the band, but on the person who you are dancing with. Your movements should complement the other person's—so you move with a sense of timing. It you don't, you'll be stepping on toes or falling over each other, and somebody's going to be looking for another partner.

So concentrate on the customer who is moving towards you and when the time is right your opening move should complement hers. The time is right when the customer has had just enough time to orient herself to the fascinating but unique CE store environment. At least fifteen seconds should pass before you contact the customer (check your watch right now and do nothing but watch fifteen seconds tick off . . . it's a longer time than you might imagine). If you approach the customer much sooner than that she will feel rushed. If she wants service in fifteen seconds or less she'll let you know. If you wait much longer than fifteen seconds when the customer is looking for help or recognition, it seems to her that she's been waiting too long. Check your watch again and watch forty-five seconds tick off . . . and then think about being in a store or department of a store where there is a gift you want to buy that you are not all that familiar with. You don't need to time yourself to get the idea that after forty-five seconds you might start feeling anxious or ignored—in either case, you need assistance right away or there is a good chance that you will turn around and leave. The fifteen/forty-five-second comfort zone is a reasonable amount of time for a greeting to take place, and it is something that you should have a natural feel for. The customer won't feel rushed and you will consequently have a better opportunity to make your first words not only heard but carry real meaning.

So let's say about twenty seconds have passed and your customer has given the store the once-over, and has one hand on the glass case where the portables are. She's tapping the glass top with her fingernails and doesn't appear to be too much at ease or that interested in the contents of the case. You approach the customer and say something.

What are you going to say? You can be pretty sure that, "Hi, how you doing today?" or "May I help you?" is not going to set any precedents in communication. So let's try some variations on these two greetings:

1. S: Hi, how are you today?
    C: I'm fine, and you?
    S: Pretty good. So what could I help you with today?
    C: I'm just looking thanks.
    S: Anything in particular?
    C: No, I'd just like to have some time to look around, if that's all right.

Let's try another variation:

2. S: So what are you doing shopping when you should be out there enjoying all the nice sunshine?
    C: Oh . . . yeah, it really is a nice day.
    S: So is there anything that I could help you with?
    C: Well right now I'd just like to look around, thanks.

What is happening? Not much more than with the original version. You either get a come-back-later or "No," or both. Starting off your sales conversation with rejection or a negative or a combination of the two is obviously not what you want to do. Now ask yourself the question I suggested earlier: "Have I said too much for the sale to happen?" Try again.

3. S: Hi.
    C: Hi . . . how are you?
    S: I'm just fine thanks, and you?
    C: I'm fine. Just sort of looking around right now.

Everything was going well until the salesperson asked a question. You greeted the customer with one word and the customer replied and asked, "How are you?" You answered the customer, and then you asked the customer a question which gave him a reasonable place to say what you didn't want to hear. Make it a rule not to ask a question in the opening stage of the sale that relates to the customer's feelings about being in the store or anything about the store. *Example*: "Have you heard the new Ultra-Linear speakers?" (*Seems like a pretty good opening line . . . now listen.*) "No I haven't. As a matter of fact, right now I'd just like to look around." *Example*: "Would you like to see the brand new Tru-Vu 2B monitor that we just got in?" (*Seems like a decent invitation, but . . .*) "Maybe later, but right now I'd just like to look around." *Example*: "So what brought you into AVC today?" (*A reasonable question, but . . .*) "We're just looking."

Here's how I would do it, remembering to ask myself, "Have I said too much for the sale to happen?"

4. S: Hi.

    C: Hi.

    S (looking out store window): That's a beautiful car you have.

    C: Thanks.

    S: That's a 944 isn't it?

    C: Yes it is.

    S: What kind of mileage do you get with a car like that, if you don't mind my asking.

    C: I really haven't checked it. I'm supposed to get somewhere in the mid-twenties, but with the gas prices the way they are now, I'm really not too concerned.

    S: Yeah, it's pretty amazing how we were paying a dollar-and-a-half a gallon a couple of weeks ago, and half that now. (*At this point you could go on to say something like,* "That's one of the things I really feel good about with home electronics. What a person can get for their money now versus a few years ago is really incredible." *At which point, you can predict a response something like,* "Oh, is that so? I was interested in taking a look at compact disc players. You carry them, don't you?" *Or, you could have said nothing after your comment on the lower price of gasoline, and would probably have got a response something like*, "Well, that's fine with me. Do you carry compact disc players?" *There is almost no chance that the customer would at that point tell you she was just looking.*)

Asking a Personalized Question

Why did the customer continue to talk to the salesperson in the last example, rather than using the cliche that spells mutual dissatisfaction and in so many words asks the salesperson to butt out? What did the salesperson do differently in the last example?

The salesperson opened up the conversation saying as little as possible and in the most pleasant way possible . . . with a smile. When the salesperson did venture to say more, what was said had nothing to do with consumer electronics. Instead, he made a complimentary remark about something that the customer was familiar with and probably proud of. The salesperson asked a sensible question with sincere interest, and dared to talk about something that was mutually and personally interesting before addressing the business at hand.

The introductory dialogue between the salesperson and the customer took less than forty-five seconds. It was certainly not a waste of time, since the salesperson didn't have to leave the customer and wait for her to browse for a few minutes and then approach the customer again hoping that she was finally ready to talk. But the forty-five seconds seemed like much longer to the customer because you tend to watch the clock less and think less about being in a strange place when you're talking about yourself—which is without a doubt almost everyone's favorite subject. That the customer felt that *more* than forty-five seconds had passed is important-. . . . Customers don't want to spend all day making their purchase, but they do want to feel that they spent some time in making a choice, rather than feeling hustled in and out.

They want to feel that you took the time to give them personal attention, and that they got their money's worth.

It's similar to going to a doctor and being attended to for less than five minutes and being charged fifty dollars. Even if the diagnosis and prescribed cure is right, you still don't feel as if you got your fifty dollars' worth. Since the customer had met a salesperson who seemed to be interested in more than a commission, she would probably be more inclined to state her needs in terms other than dollars. And it is a nice irony that bigger commissions are forthcoming with more personalized sales approaches. I think we've all found ourselves in situations where we were unfamiliar with an item that we were buying. If you were a man buying a gift in the ladies' accessories department, wouldn't you spend more on a purse for your wife or girlfriend if you found a salesperson who was friendly, who made a point of letting you know that it was a pleasure to help you choose a gift for someone who was special, and then proceeded to ask you some thoughtful questions which would help you make a good choice?

If you ask the customer about something that has more to do with the customer than with the store, you get a positive response. *Example*: "Oh, a Nikon! I just bought an FX-8. How do you like yours?" (*A question that the customer can easily relate to, and possibly even share a mutual interest. Could the customer say "Just looking" and sound rational? Just listen.*) "Oh a Nikon! I just bought an FX-8. How do you like yours?" "Right now, I'm just looking." (*At what—cameras?*) If you don't want to hear someone rejecting you in four words or less, don't set them up for it. The right questions to ask will, of course, depend upon the customer.

Here are some examples of other personalized questions that cannot be answered dismissively with, "Just looking," or, "No," and which will initiate a brief conversation that will give the customer a chance to get oriented, or just get comfortable....

"That's a great looking jacket. What kind of leather is that?"

(Looking at the record store bag...) "So what new records did you buy today?"

"Your baby is sure cute. What's her name?"
"Who's on the cover this month?"
"Nice sunglasses. Where did you get them?"
"What are you reading?"
"Where did you buy your Walkman?"
(Looking at a frozen yogurt...) "What's your favorite flavor?"

The customers bring in the right questions with them; they are part of the question. Asking a customer how he likes his camera or what her favorite flavor of frozen yogurt is is not getting too personal. They wouldn't be carrying it around with them if they didn't mind someone's noticing. Remember the woman who drove up in the 944? She didn't buy a car like that to be anonymous; compliments like the salesperson just gave her were included in the price.

One word of caution, though, in making personal comments or asking personalized questions: make sure that you like what you're highlighting. Phony shows through. And it's hard to be nice and feel like it if you don't really feel it! But if you're a keen observer, you can find something positive about almost everyone. Think about yourself... it wouldn't be worth getting up in the morning if there weren't at least one thing about yourself that was worth a compliment.

On that note, let's go back to the dance for a moment. You usually don't do the splits and a backbend as your opening step. You usually try to find the beat and get a feeling for the melody, and get in synch with your partner before doing the Travolta tango. You do the same thing with the customer. And for the moment, the customer is your partner in this sequence of moves called the magic sell. So pay some attention to your partner, the customer, before taking the stage and unfolding the bigger-than-life world of CE. You certainly have the time, because it saves you the time you would otherwise spend waiting to begin all over again.

With the nicest or the most seasoned of customers, a simple greeting—"Hi" or "Hello," minus the "How are you?"—followed by an appropriate personal comment or personalized question, will convert what the customer thought would be an interview or confrontation into a simple conversation. And it will be well worth your time and the customer's time. The answer to our question—"Have I said too much for the sale to happen?"—is a matter of listening. You can't say too much as long as the customer is talking. The customer will generally make the leap from incidental talk to home-entertainment talk without your guidance, and it will usually take less than a minute to go from the leather jacket to, "What kind of dubbing decks do you guys carry?"

If the customer proves to be the exception and is looking for a conversation partner rather than a conversant salesperson, you can get the customer on track very easily by asking the one question that you would never normally ask: "So what can I help you with?" If the customer is looking for more than company, he will get to the specifics. If he's looking for a friend, he'll say something like, "Oh, I think I'll just take a look around. Don't let me keep you." Excuse yourself and, who knows, with time on your side, that person might eventually find something really worth talking about—and you can bet that he'll be sure to buy it from you, the first person who paid a little special attention.

Using the Silent Question and the Way-To-Go Approach

Another communication technique which I have found to be very effective during this step of the sale, as well as later on, is the silent question. That's right. Saying nothing and looking as though you're expecting something will—at the right time and place—gets you more information than a half-dozen questions. Just say "Hi" or "Good evening" and smile. When the customers say "Hi" in reply, restrain yourself from saying anything. Just smile and look at them expectantly. Remember that it was the customers who came to see you . . . they have some pretty specific concerns and a mission, otherwise they would not have made a special trip. Within a second or two most people will succumb to their natural social tendencies, and feel the need to say something to establish their identity in a strange place, and in doing so will tell you more than they had originally intended. If they have a specific item in mind they will often ask you where they can find it. You simply say, "Follow me," and then proceed to ask them a few key questions before showing it to them.

Or let's take the case of a couple. When you say "Hi" and they say "Hi" and you are quiet and smiling with a bright expectant look, they'll look at each other and —with a couple of silent gestures that mean, "You tell him . . . No, *you* tell him . . . Okay, let's *both* tell him"—and within a matter of seconds, both of them will be blurting out the reason why they came to see you. One of them says, "Okay, you tell him." And the designated spokesperson starts telling you that they have this little cabin where they seem to be spending more time, and they have a couple of speakers and a receiver, and they were thinking that a cassette deck would. . . . And you listen and nod your head as you lead the way towards the cassette decks, ready to suggest a variety of portable and home cassette deck combinations.

It is with this technique that your respect for the ninety-three percent of your communication ability is critical. I'm asking you to use the silent question for another reason other than the fact that it works. This is a very real test of the kind of first impression you are making. It is your ability to control the sound of the first word out of your mouth and the look on your face that will make this technique effective. If you are the first person to break the silence after the customer says "Hi" in reply, then it would be advisable to review the preparatory steps which will give you the confidence to communicate non-verbally in a friendly and effective manner. We will be using the silent question at other times as we continue to explore the seven-step approach to selling. . . . It's hard to listen when you're talking. . . . More on that later.

Of course, there is the chance that the customer may look back at you and say, "Could we just look around?" This is your first opportunity to say "Yes"—that short and sweet affirmative—also your first opportunity to ask another question, which is a technique in itself. It's called the Way-to-Go approach. The operative question for this approach is an exception to the rule, because either "Yes" or "No" is the right answer, and provides a way for you to continue talking with the customer.

S: Hi.
C: Hi.
(Brief silence.)
C: Could we just look around?
S: Yes, you certainly may. Have you ever been to AVC before?

(Remember, the answer to this question will work for you whether the customer says "Yes" or "No." If the customer says "No," you will say something like, "Well, welcome to our store. It's always a pleasure to meet a new customer. Let me take just a few seconds and tell you where everything is . . ." *And you proceed to take a minute to vocally map out the store for them, and tell them where they can find all of the major component categories. The chances are very high that before you finish, he will stop you at the component which he is specifically interested in, and ask you where exactly he can find that particular item. You can then say,* "Just follow me. It's right over here. . . ." *And show him the way-to-go to his desired product or system.)*
Now let's play the other side:

S: Hi.
C: Hi.
(Brief silence.)
S: I think I'll just take a look around.
C: Please do. Have you been to AVC before?
S: Yes. *(Here you'll want to say something similar to,* "Great, it's always a pleasure to meet an old customer. What was it that you bought?" *(After finding out the nature of his purchase if he made one, be sure and ask who his salesperson was. If the customer remembers or if the other salesperson is available, reintroduce the customer to his former salesperson.*

If the customer is clearly yours, proceed to ask how he is enjoying what ever it is that he bought, and ask what he is looking for today. If the customer is specific, show him the way. If the customer just wants to browse, and it's been a while since he was last in, you might want to tell him that: "The store has been changed

around quite a bit since the last time you were in. Let me take a few seconds and tell you where everything is . . . "
Again, you use the way-to-go approach, and the return customer will probably stop you on a specific before you get past two component categories. The return customer wants to feel like a preferred customer, and will probably want to secure your personal attention almost immediately.

We've talked a lot about the "Just-looking" response, and ways to avoid it, but that doesn't mean that the customer should never be allowed to browse or walk the floor unaccompanied. It does mean, however, that millions of CE customers go into stores and just look, and that's about all, and that's not the way you satisfy customers. Less "Just-looking" means more satisfied customers. But when you do find an occasion to encourage the customer to browse, be sure to exchange names (when you give yours, ask for the customer's . . . that's key to making your next contact). Let the customer know that if he or she has any questions you will be glad to answer them.

When a person says "Just looking," it is very important that you don't look disappointed. Remain bright, confident, and friendly. Don't let your level of enthusiasm drop even one decibal . . . and this is not easy when you have worked hard towards starting up some communication and a person comes up with an automatic, nonsensical "Just looking." Be positive, and look as if that's just what you wanted the customer to say. Say, "Great. Take your time. My name is . . . " and put yourself at his disposal. And *do not turn and walk away*, because it is your store and the customer is the one who wants to do the looking. If you linger, the customer might just say, "Oh, before you go, could you tell me where you keep the car stereos?" "Just follow me," you reply, turning and walking towards the car stereo display. Way-to-go!

STEP FOUR:
Listening As the Only Way to Get to Know Your Customer

Listening As the Only Way to Get to Know Your Customers

THE FIRST THING that you should do you at this step of the sale is to ask questions which will get a communication started and keep it going in the right direction. Somebody has to say something if you or the customer are going to have something to listen to other than the equipment. During this step of the sale, you and the customer are going to be talking about what brought the customer into the store. It's time to let the customer tell you what he or she wants, and give you the background which you will need. How you get this information and how you handle it will determine the customer's level of satisfaction. It will determine whether the customer leaves feeling satisfied, i.e., makes a purchase worth talking about.

I've said it before and I will say it again ... and again. Selling something is the only way you can satisfy the customer, *but* it is also possible to sell something and have the customer walk away unsatisfied. That's the difference between selling and the magic sell—the difference between satisfaction and mutual satisfaction—the difference between a job as a CE salesperson and a career as a successful CE sales professional.

Five Factors of Satisfaction

You assume that the customers came into your store to buy something. Your assumption is correct. Whether they do or do not buy depends upon five factors which are critical concerns of the customer—and all are within your control. These are the five factors of satisfaction:

1. Finding a salesperson who enjoys what he or she is doing and who therefore looks good and comes across as the friendly, credible person the customer has been looking to do business with.
2. Finding a salesperson who is patient and sensitive enough to find out their needs as accurately as they can describe them.
3. Finding a salesperson who is knowledgeable enough to clarify their needs and give them a good idea of what they're buying, given their own limited information and background.
4. Finding a salesperson who will make sure that the customers get their money's worth, whether they have the equivalent of six month's-worth of allowances, a thousand-dollar budget, or a "Money-is-no-object" attitude. (In the latter case, money may not be a main concern, but the fact that they get their money's worth still is.)
5. Finding a salesperson who validates his or her store as the best place to make the purchase and presents real service advantages as proof of this.

Looking at the fifth factor, what is the main advantage? Right. The main advantage is you. Which takes you back to the first factor which is something we've talked about and which you must never forget. Come up short on number one and you won't have to worry about the other four, because you won't have a customer.

Upon reviewing the five factors of satisfaction, what is the one thing you can do more than anything else that will assist you in addressing all five areas of your customer's concern?

If you said "Listen," you're right. Improving your listening skills will of course effect greater customer satisfaction. It can't help but help you and the customer communicate better. Consider for a moment—a very brief moment—how you would fare by listening less. Just a moment's consideration of that possibility should be enough to get the point. You're actually asking yourself how you would feel about communicating less. And your job, as a CE sales professional, does not allow for that possibility.

Now let's take a careful look at the second factor of satisfaction. *Finding a salesperson who is patient and sensitive enough to find out their needs as accurately as they can describe them.* It's true that patience and sensitivity are not subject to automatic command any more than a good attitude or being nice is, but what is one of the most noticeable attributes of someone you would call patient and sensitive? The ability to listen. When someone tells you that someone else is a "good listener," you automatically feel more comfortable with the person even before meeting. You get a positive feeling about the person, and you're eager to meet him or her. But how do you feel when a person tells you that someone is "Quite a talker," or, "Can really talk up a storm?" Are you eager to meet that person or are you a little apprehensive?

The good listener also has the good sense to know that listening is not just a nice thing to do, or a way to put people at ease, but is the only way to learn something about someone else. And that is what the second factor of satisfaction is all about. Finding out the customers' needs as accurately as *they can describe them.* That means the customer is going to be doing a lot of the talking and you're going to have to do some good listening. It also means that you are going to have to help the customer out. Customers just don't walk into a strange environment and start spilling out every pertinent detail relating to the purchase of a camcorder. However, if you've adequately prepared yourself and take the time to greet your customer as a person rather than just another consumer, your customer is going to feel more comfortable about needing your help. . . .)

Customers tend to talk in general terms and salespeople tend to accept the generalizations as facts. Example:

> C: We'd like to look at your televisions.
> S: Certainly. Right this way.
> (Leads the customers to the televisions.)

S: Did you have anything special in mind?

C: Well something better than what we have now.

S: Let me show you the new XO-L8 monitor. It's quite a set.

It's going to have to be quite a set! In fact, it should be a small screen, big screen, portable, console, dual speaker, remote control, stereo broadcast ready, equipped with direct A/V jacks, a digital clock, sleep timer, and, of course, you should be able to plug it into your cigarette lighter and also take it to football games with you in case you have an extra ticket. If all you know about the customers' needs is that they want a television set better than the one they currently have, and if that's going to be your information base, you had better find a set that is all things to all people. The only problem is that it doesn't exist.

This may seem to be stretching the point, but think back to the time you shopped your competition. You probably won't find it hard to remember the times you were shown a piece of equipment because the salesperson either had a personal preference—or else was clairvoyant. After all, he must have been, because the salesperson's choice was certainly not based on anything you said—you weren't allowed to say much of anything. Example:

C: I'm looking for a car stereo.

S: No problem. Let me show you some.

Have you seen that happen? And the customer leaves twenty minutes later with twenty different prices on decks, equalizers, power boosters, and speakers. It's a free game that CE stores have been handing out for a number of years now. It's called "Mix and Match Your Favorite Component" ... in the privacy of the customer's own home where he'll never have to worry about spending money or buying something he wants. Confusion is a pretty good cure for even the most enthusiastic of shoppers. And it doesn't take too much "mixing and matching" to get overloaded with confusion.

The game is certainly not exclusive to the CE industry. As a matter of fact, it's traditional to almost all forms of retail.

Have you ever walked into a used car lot and told the salesperson that you were looking for a good reliable car, and before
you knew it you were sitting behind the wheel of a Batmobile,
being told that, "This little baby will do zero-to-sixty in less
than nine seconds and not only do you deserve something
that's got a little pizzazz, but you *owe* it to yourself when you
can get speed, excitement and reliability like this for less than
nine thousand dollars?" The salesperson might have a very
good point, but his preference and instinct prevailed over his
common sense. You just want to get out of that car and go
someplace where it's safe. Someplace where they hear what
you say, or at least give you a chance to fill in the blanks.

Evaluative listening

There are all kinds of televisions, car stereos, and good reliable
cars, and the customer has the right to make a decision based
upon experience and expertise rather than on bias and ignorance. Bias and ignorance are not something that any of the
salespeople in these scenarios would admit to. Maybe they
didn't do what they did on purpose (we all know how strong a
defense that is). If they didn't, then they should take the time
to do a few things on purpose that will do someone some good.

Number one . . . when the customers said they wanted a
television, and when the salesperson asked if the customers
had anything special in mind and then found out that the
customers wanted something better than they currently had,
the salesperson could have listened and *listened in a very
special way.*

Let's do it again.

C: We'd like to look at your televisions.
S: Certainly. Right this way.
(Leads customers to the televisions.)
S: Did you have anything special in mind?
C: Well, something better than what we have now.

Rather than rushing off to show his customers the new
XO-L8—no matter how great a set it may be—what should the
salesperson ask? That's right. If the salesperson is going to

show them something better than they have now, he had better find out what the customers have now. The customers may have been living with a 13″ black-and-white set or may have gotten tired of focusing the red and green rays of their 48″ big screen. In either case, it is important to find that out.

The most efficient way of doing that is to use a form of listening that is called *evaluative* listening. You listen to what the customers have just said ... you listen for details and accuracy ... and you also listen with an ear towards judging any assumptions and conclusions which they may make. You listen to find out where they're going with what they're saying.

To evaluate what is being said, you use the five-"W" questions. These are questions that begin with *What, Who, Where, When, Why,* and (one "H") *How,* and are almost impossible to answer intelligently with a simple yes or no. (For instance: "Did you go out last night?" "Yes." And that could be the end of the conversation. Now add a word: "Where did you go out last night?" And you'll probably not only find out where, but who with, when, and what they did.)

If you now refer back to the personalized questions used to greet the customers, you will notice that most of those questions were directed towards "What," "Who," or "Where." Journalists and psychologists—people whose livelihood depends upon listening and getting more than a yes or no answer—have used evaluative listening for years. Now lets return to the TV customers:

> S: Did you have anything special in mind?
> C: Well, certainly something better than we have now.
> S: What kind of TV do you have now?
> C: It's an older set. A Tru-Vu.
> S: Tru-Vu makes nice televisions. How long have you had it?
> C: Oh gosh, we've probably had it for about eight-nine years.
> S: Well, it's given you good service in the meantime, I would suppose. So what are you looking for in a new set?

C: A decent picture for one thing.

S: You're looking for a nice clear, crisp picture. And what kind of special features would you like?

C: We want remote control...and we've heard about all this cable-ready stuff and stereo and it gets pretty confusing. Maybe you could tell us a little bit about it.

S: I'd be glad to. That way you can let me know exactly what you want. Do you own a VCR?

C: No. That's something else we'd like to find out about.

S: I'd be happy to tell you anything you need to know. Let me just ask you a couple more questions, and then I'd like to tell you about some of the exciting features you'll find on the new sets, and I'll also be able to give you an idea of how these features can benefit you personally.

How would you feel if you were the customer in the above exchange? Pretty good, I would imagine. That conversation lasted less than a minute—but again, it probably seemed longer to the customers. That made the customers feel good, because someone was paying attention to them while they talked about their personal concerns. How did the salesperson listen? He used evaluative listening, and also *active* listening—which we will get to in a moment.

He asked what kind of TV they have, for the obvious but often overlooked reasons cited before. He made a comment on Tru-Vu that told the customers he heard what they were saying as soon as they had said it. *Someone's listening.* He figuratively patted the old set on the back rather than dismissing it as a worthless piece of junk. The customers feel that they made a good choice in the past, and will feel more confident about making a decision now.

Rather than immediately tossing a remote control to the customers, he asked *what* they were looking for in a new set.When they voiced their main concern, which was pretty general, he responded with a reflective statement and made the general a little bit more specific. When he said, "... nice clear, crisp picture," he let the customers hear what they had said in more vivid and exact terms. If a price objection should come up later on, he can always remind them of one of the factors that they specified from the very first, and which they will now remember as "a nice clear, crisp picture."

He went on to ask *what* kind of special features they were looking for, and they told him what they knew and how much they didn't know. He probably wouldn't have got much of a reading had he asked, "Are you looking for any special features?" It would be too easy to say "No" or "I don't know"—and had one of them said "Yes," it would have meant asking two questions when one question would have worked better. That's called economy of movement—in this case involving words— and is something that professionals in any field work at daily.

He offered to give advice, but was not tempted to become a fount of information or elaborate on the idea of buying a television yet—it wasn't the right time. There were other things to find out first, like, "Did they own a VCR?" or would they like to? By asking that question at the first, rather than at the end, of the sale, there is a pretty good chance that they will own one before they leave. It's not only what you ask, and how you ask it, but also when you ask it. Your sense of timing is one of the main things that differentiates a good salesperson from just another person on the floor. That's why the magic sell is a step-by-step approach rather than just another run for the money. And wouldn't you rather help your customers carry out a TV and a VCR rather than just the TV that represents only half of the great idea of video? Sometimes how much a person buys is a pretty good indicator of their level of satisfaction.

He offers his services again, but lets the customers know that there are still a couple of questions that he needs to ask. This makes the customers feel as important as they should feel, and it also lets a little anticipation build up prior to the presentation.

Then the salesperson makes a promise to tell the customers about some exciting new features and in seventeen words goes on to say something else with an unusual sense of clarity. This phrase is one that every salesperson should know by rote: " . . . I'll also be able to give you an idea of how those features can benefit you personally." That's exactly what the customers want to hear—and it is also a very neat way of reminding yourself of what you have to do if your presentation is going to make the necessary good impression on the customers. You are going to tell the customers about the features, explain or demonstrate the benefit or the idea of the feature, and then, based upon what you find out about the customers, *personalize* the *benefit* of the *feature*.

If you use that phrase with every customer, every customer will know why he is buying what you are selling, and what it will do for him personally. He will know why it is a good idea especially for him. We will be talking a lot about this during Step Five.

Were the customers listening? Yes, otherwise they couldn't have answered the questions. Was the salesperson listening? Yes, otherwise he could not have made a relevant comment on everything that was said, and then ask a question that was always in synch with a plan of action. Did the customers *know* the salesperson was listening? Yes, because he made reflective statements that summarized what the customers had said, or asked evaluative questions that prompted the customers to listen and respond rather than get mesmerized by a wall of thirty TV's tuned to the same channel.

The salesperson said he wanted to ask just a couple more questions before talking about special features. That meant there were still things he was listening for and hadn't heard yet. What do you suppose some of those questions would be? Refer back to that one-minute conversation—and then close the book and think about what kind of questions you might want to ask the customers at this point.

Now let's listen in:

> S: When do you usually watch TV?
>
> C: I watch quite a bit at night when I get home from work, and my wife watches some daytime TV.
>
> S: And where are you going to be putting the new television?
>
> C: We just built on a new room, which is sort of a combination entertainment and guest room.
>
> S: That's certainly a good reason for considering a VCR. How large is the room?
>
> C: It's a pretty good size. About twelve by fifteen.
>
> S: That's a very nice room. Whereabouts in the room are you planning on putting the new TV?
>
> C: We've had cabinets and shelves built all along one wall. That's where we were planning on putting the TV and the stereo.
>
> S: Oh, so actually you're going to have a full-fledged audio-video room. What kind of stereo do you have?
>
> C: We bought it from AVC several years ago. It's got a turntable, cassette deck. The whole works. Still sounds great.

That took about forty-five seconds, so the salesperson has now spent less than two minutes with the customers. But given the quality of information which the salesperson got, don't you get the feeling that there is a much better chance that they will buy, rather than shop and disappear?

The questions that the salesperson asked did not drop out of the blue. They were based upon what he heard. The questions enabled him to find out what his customers really wanted when they said they wanted to take a look at televisions.

He asked when they watch TV. Why was that important? To find out if their lifestyle demands a special need for time-shifting, which would of course make a better case for purchasing a VCR. When the salesperson gives his summary, he will ask the couple if there are daytime programs that they might miss, and tell them that this is no longer a problem; he will also mention the thirty-minute auto-record feature to them.

By asking where the couple was going to put it, he found out the real reason why they were looking at televisions, and opened up a whole brand new world of possibilities which also said a lot about what kind of investment they would be making and how soon the purchase would be. Later on in the sale, the salesperson may have reason to remind the customer that the room is not an entertainment room until the TV and VCR arrive. And since that's what they built the room for, well . . .

Why ask about the size of the room? Well, since it's pretty large, the salesperson will tell the customer that it makes sense to have a larger rather than smaller screen and then they will really be able to appreciate the "nice clear, crisp" picture that they said they wanted. And wanting remote really makes sense, he will tell them, since in a room that large, you don't want to be jumping up and down all the time changing channels. You want to sit back and relax and let the wireless do the walking. To fill that large a room, they will also want dual-speakers, even if they do end up combining the stereo with the TV. There are times when you just want to listen to the television and not make a big production about it, but you still want clear, high-quality sound which dual speakers will give them in a larger size room.

Where in the room will they be putting the TV? Getting a little too specific, maybe? Next thing, he'll be asking how many inches off the ground they'll be sitting. But the customers didn't mind one bit. Matter of fact, they were happy to tell him about the shelves and cabinets that stretch all the way down that wall. They're proud of it. And, in a couple of minutes, the salesperson will tell them why he's showing them a big-screen monitor that will fit on their shelves rather than a console that would require another remodel and, once again, prove that he was listening—for the good of the customer—and himself. And, he also found out that they had a stereo.

Upon finding out about the stereo, the salesperson puts it all together for the customers in one sentence. Now they not only have an entertainment room, but soon they will have an "A/V room" and be telling their friends about it.

Everything that the salesperson asked was for a good reason. And every answer that the customers gave was responded to—and validated the worth of the question in the first place. Now when the salesperson proceeds to tell them about the special features, he won't assume the role of an operator's manual and review every feature of every TV. He knows what they need—specifically, and, even more important, knows what they can use in a more general sense. The VCR has now assumed a more important role in the scheme of the A/V room concept—which has just been introduced to the customer like a dream they never knew they had.

Listening is not part of the process of discovering the customer's needs, and getting to know the customers. Listening *is* the process.

It's now pretty clear that when you ask a question, you ask it for a reason. Casual conversation may be appropriate when first meeting and getting to know the customer, but there is really no point in talking about the weather or the newest thing in running shoes when it is time to get an idea of what the customer's needs are. Let's take a look at some other five-"W" evaluative questions which you will find yourself using on a regular basis, and then let's listen to what the question can tell you about what the customer wants and what the customer should have.

What kind of system (for system substitute television, or the requested component, when appropriate) do you have now?
If you're going to suggest an improvement, you had better know what the customer currently owns or had,

or what level of quality she is accustomed to. You want to pinpoint the customer's needs. Don't play darts in the dark.

What systems have you seen (and heard) that you really like?

The answer to this question will give you the general parameters of what the customer wants and expects in a system of his own. You then have to determine whether the customer's expectations are reasonable. The customer may be thinking of a friend's system that was purchased ten years ago which still stands as the model by which all other systems are measured. Or the system may be the one seen at a Grateful Dead concert utilizing two or three hundred drivers and a battery of amplifiers. In either case, you get a better idea of what the customer expects the system to look like and sound like. Or the system may be the one you advertised last week. And you get an exact idea of what the customer wants.

Where did you see the system?

You may have already got the answer to this question with the preceding question. It's most useful if the customer describes a system made up of current products which you do not carry. You will learn where the customer has been shopping, and if you know your competition, you now have a nice advantage.

What things impressed you most about that system?

The answer will tell you what to show the customer in lieu of the products that you don't carry, and what features and aspects of the equipment you should be focusing on.

What was there that you didn't like about the system?

You should probably get some indication as to why the customer is still waiting to buy.

How often do you buy records (... CD's, videos, or

rent videos, or how often do you record)?

This is when the customer expresses her priorities, which also gives you a pretty good idea of how much the customer is willing to invest.

May I ask where you live, because that will give me an idea of what kind of FM reception you've been getting...or tell me what kind of cable system you're using....

And knowing where the customer lives will also give you a better idea of the customer's income level.

Who is going to be using the system the most?

This can tell you whether durability or convenience is a special consideration, and, more important, whether all decision-makers are present.

Remember that the answers to these and other questions are only important if we are listening. If you find yourself thinking about what kind of pizza you're going to have after work while the customer tells you about his friend's system that has this turntable with a marble base and speakers that are big enough to live in, you're wasting the time and energy of both the customer and yourself. If you find yourself already thinking of something else that you would like to ask the customer, you are there where you should be—listening, ready to do the customer and yourself a favor. By choosing the right product for the right person, you will have a satisfied customer who will be back for more, rather than just another buyer and one more invoice.

Before reviewing the various methods of listening which we have seen used, let's look at another thing that the salesperson was able to do by concentrating on listening.

The questions followed each other in a logical manner. I mean "logical" as in a conversation. Here's an example that you've all experienced:

S: It's really a nice day out today, isn't it?
C: Yeah, it's almost like summer.

Nothing wrong with that, now how about this:

> S: It's really a nice day out today, isn't it?
> C: Yeah, these televisions get bigger every day don't they?

Doesn't quite follow, but you've all experienced similar conversations. Someone is not getting through, or one person is not listening. But that conversation is no more illogical than this one:

> C: We're certainly looking for something better than we have now.
> S: Let me show you the new XO-L8 monitor.

In neither case was the input of the other party really considered. One person talked and then another person talked—without listening. The customers who are about to equip their A/V room didn't have this problem. The sequence of questions followed their line of thinking, and led them to possibilities that they were not previously aware of.

During your next conversation, on or off the floor, start practicing evaluative listening. Start asking *where did you go, when did you do that, what did that mean, why did he say that, how did you know, who was that?* See how long you can keep a conversation going with just minimal comments from yourself. It's amazing how easy it is, and you'll wonder why you haven't done it more when you see that smile of self-satisfaction spread across the face of the person who has just said more to you in one sitting than during the entire time he's known you. I said *when you see,* and it's true that when you're listening you also have time to look at the other person and see him in a brighter light than when you were glancing through the blur of your own message. Getting to know another person means giving a person enough time to be himself. Once you've done that for him, he'll be happy to listen to you—and he'll be listening with a smile rather than with squinted eyes and a face turned slightly to one side as though he were getting ready to dodge another jab to the head.

If you practice evaluative listening with your friends, you'll be doing them a real favor—and doing yourself a favor too, because soon this form of listening will become second nature. The next time you're introduced to a new person, make it a point to ask several things about the other person before you say anything about yourself. You'll be surprised at what a fascinating person you can become by talking less and listening more.

Active Listening

I've also mentioned something called active listening. As the salesperson starts becoming more specific in pointing the customers towards their needs for an audio/video system, he will use active listening as a technique. He will be able to use it because of what he found out with the more direct evaluative listening technique. When the time comes to tell the couple about the thirty-minute instant record feature, or about the programmable recording features, or that the big screen doesn't come only in a console cabinet and that their shelves are still a worthwhile part of the new room . . . when the time comes to remind a person of his needs and give him an idea of the features, or to provide positive feedback, *and the time is still not right for your personal opinion,* use active listening! It will serve you well. This, of course, depends upon the degree of evaluative listening that was done—if very little, then you are forced to give your opinion since that's about all you have as an information base. And, of course, your opinion only serves to confirm that you have an opinion, and so does everyone else. The currency of your opinion decreases in value the more often that it's used.

A more immediately usable and equally effective variation of active listening relies upon your being quiet and identifying the feeling behind what was said and then summarizing that feeling in words similar to the ones you just heard. Probably one of the most vivid examples of this occuring was during your first important date. That's when you met the person who finally really "understood." Let's take another little trip back in time. . . .

You've just finished off two bags of fries and concluded a ten minute story of some wild and crazy thing that you did by saying something like, "Well, it probably isn't such a big deal, but I don't really see why they had to ground me for a whole week for doing something that half the school was doing."

And the other person might have said something like, "Yeah, maybe you were just grounded for a week, but it probably really seemed unfair to be punished for something that almost everybody else was doing too."

And you responded, "Yeah, that's it exactly. I mean, why should I be singled out for doing something that wasn't that weird or anything? And then right after that, during next semester, I'm tooling down Wrigley Drive with a bunch of other guys and out pops this . . . " And ten minutes later you conclude by saying something like, "I mean, taking my keys away for two weeks wasn't like the end of the world or anything, but like I wasn't the only sophomore that ever drove fifty miles an hour in a twenty-five mile zone."

And the other person responded with, "Two weeks can really seem like a long time. And it hurts when you're treated like you're the only person that ever made a mistake."

And again you respond, "Exactly! That's it exactly. And I mean that was just the beginning. Next semester and guess what happens?"

The other person who by now really, I mean really, understands. says, "What?" and you're off on another story about life on a ten-speed in the fast lane. And you keep talking until the other person mentions something about being tired. And you understand, because the other person understands you so well.

If you were the person doing the talking in the above instance, why would you feel the other person understood? Why would you feel a high degree of trust in the other person? Where did this giant rush of rapport come from? The other person said less than twenty-five words in each response, as compared to literally thousands of words by yourself.

Are we to conclude, then, that trust and rapport is a result of a few words? Not really. What if the other person's first response had been, "Wow, you were lucky to only get a week. I did something that wasn't half as bad as that and got grounded for a month!" That would have been a personal challenge which would have added to your own frustration when you were trying to come to some kind of fair conclusion, and looking for a little bit of sympathy. The spotlight would have also been refocused onto the person with the lesser offense and harsher punishment.

That person's response would have been something like saying, "Big deal," without regard for how you felt about what you had just said. Instead, the person said, "Yeah, maybe you were just grounded for a week, but it probably really seemed unfair to be punished for something that almost everybody else was doing too." The person wanted to get to know you rather than "letting you know what they thought"—as in opinion. The person merely accepted what you had concluded and how you felt about it—frustrated—and fed it back to you with the same feeling using slightly different words. At the time it seemed like the right and natural thing to do. And I'm sure that you thought it was. There was no judgment made, no advice, no presumptions—just a matter of reiterating, and allowing you to hear your own conclusion again—essentially, the person confirmed what you had said by repeating what you had said. And that was enough to keep you going; someone just said, "I'm listening," at a time in your life when that was very important. But let me ask you something: is there a time in your life when listening isn't important?

Doing your best to understand someone is what active listening is all about. Have you ever used any of the following phrases? "What was that you said?" "Run that by me again." "I didn't quite understand the last part of what you said." "What do you mean?" "Could you please repeat that?" If you have used any of them—and not to challenge but to clarify— you are acquainted with active listening. And nobody minds repeating themselves once if it means that someone else is going to understand what they said in the first place.

There is usually a follow-up phrase to the above phrases.

Something like the following: "Oh, so what you're saying is...." "So if I've got this right, what you're saying is...." "Okay what I hear you saying is...." Or, the most famous of them all: "In other words...." Unfortunately, too often the "other words" impart another meaning which is closer to what the listener wanted to hear than what the speaker wanted to say.

As a personal exercise, the next time you hear yourself using one of these phrases, make a conscious effort to say what you heard the other person saying rather than what you would have liked them to say. Your lesson in listening integrity will more than pay for itself. You'll hear the other person saying, "Exactly!" rather than, "No, not exactly—what I was really saying was...." Too often, communications are stifled and sabotaged in the name of clarification. By the time the person says what he really meant to say, the time is past for it to have any real impact. You can only say what you mean so many times before you are doing a kind of unconscious self-parody, or saying what someone else means for you to say.

Too many salespeople have taken phrases that were supposedly aimed at clarifying something, and have used enough "other words" until the original phrase is affirming something that the customer is still confused by or thinks of in a negative way. Have you ever heard a conversation that goes something like this?

C: I really feel that's more than we want to spend.

S: Oh, so what you're saying is, you like what you see, but it costs too much.

C: No, actually we were looking at ... or at least *thought* we were looking, at something that costs about half that.

S: So what you're saying is that when you saw what you really liked, you were a little bit over your budget, but don't worry—that's why I'm here. To take care of problems like that. So if I can do something about the price of the XO-L8 system, you'd consider it. Is that what you're saying?

And, of course, by this time the customers don't know

what they are saying and have only a vague notion of what the salesperson is saying, so while they try to straighten out the communications end, the salesperson goes running off to the manager in search of the biggest discount of the day. And when the customers are presented with the equivalent of a $250 floor rebate, they feel more than a little impelled to consider it. The customers buy a system they're really not sure of and the store sells a thousand-dollars' worth of merchandise at close to cost.

And whose fault is it? It isn't the fault of the customers, who are now being accused of grinding the salesperson. It's the salesperson's fault. He doesn't know how, or even *care*, about listening. He is busy being cunning, rather than clever. Confusing rather than clear. This salesperson isn't concerned about being nice. He feels he doesn't have the time to be nice. He's under pressure—which is a more accurate way of describing what is usually called "high pressure." His is a conscious attempt to sell to the customer without regard for the customer's needs. Those are the "tactics" of the salesperson who should have caught the last used car out of town, but unfortunately is still sticking around. Mutual satisfaction has never really been this person's concern, having never taken the time to experience it.

Listening not only takes concentration and hard work, but means being conscientious and concerned about another person's needs. The common ground is your concern for communicating so that you can effect mutual satisfaction. Finding the common ground is how the magic sell happens.

Responsive Listening

We have talked about evaluative listening and active listening. There is one other method of listening which will allow you to facilitate more effective communication with your customer. Remember my mentioning "economy of movement" as related to the efficient use of words? If you understood how significantly this would improve your overall sales effectiveness, you will be especially interested in responsive listening, which allows you to get very specific information by using a single word.

It's not hard to learn. It just takes a sensitive ear, and the same good sense of timing as do the other methods of listening which we've discussed. Let me give you an example:

> During a conversation with a friend, he says, "We're going to the Caribbean with my brother-in-law this winter for our vacation."

> If I reply, "We?" he will explain, "Yeah, the whole family. I think it'll be even more fun with the kids."

> If I reply, "Brother-in-law?" he will elaborate, "Yeah. We've been spending quite a bit of time with him and his family. We get along real well, so it should be a lot of fun for everybody.

> If I reply, "Caribbean?" he will explain, "Yeah, we decided to do it right this year. We've been to Hawaii the last couple of years, and so we decided to do something different. And the kids and everybody really deserve it."

> If I reply, "Vacation," he will say, "Damn right. Vacation. And it's about time. For the first time in years I'm taking a full two weeks. Maybe three, who knows."

The method is obvious, and anybody who has ever had a job interview can attest to its validity. The personnel manager looks at your application and says, "It says here, 'mountain climbing.'" "That's right," you say. "I like to get away from the city when I get the time. The eastern slope of the Sierra is where I generally go, or Yosemite—past Tuolume, if you're familiar with that part of the country..." The personnel manager nods her head, smiles, and proceeds to pick another word or phrase up from your application and show it to you for whatever you think it's worth. And it's usually worth at least twenty-five times more words than she used.

The interview ends and she's had a good opportunity to listen to you, watch your expressions, and test your reactions to things which she found noteworthy. And you felt it was a good interview, because you certainly had a chance to tell her about some things that you felt were important. Or was she the one who felt important? And maybe you felt important because you were given the opportunity to talk about one of the most important people you know—you.

It's not difficult to see why this technique is also used by therapists and journalists: "Mr. President! You said, 'With deliberation.'" "Yes Bob. I said, 'with deliberation,' and I hope you people won't construe what I said this afternoon to mean anything but...."

It's easy to see why this would be an excellent technique for you to use with customers. Simply focus on the key word, or words. Repeat it with a questioning tone and wait for the customer to give you the desired information on the topic you specified. "I like speakers that have a lot of punch," says the customer. "A lot of punch?" you reply. "Yeah, I like to listen to rock 'n' roll," says the customer. "And I like to play it like it should really sound. It's gotta really have that..." And you suddenly have a much better idea of what speakers you're going to be demonstrating.

Again, practice on the people you know best, and then use it with your customers to enhance your job satisfaction and your income. You'll be doing everybody a favor.

The EAR Method of Listening

An easy way for you to refer to the three methods of listening which you will be using—*E*valuative listening, *A*ctive listening and *R*esponsive listening—is to remember that they stand for EAR. Of course, you know by now that it takes more than a good ear to listen. Listening to get to know your customer or anyone else takes concentration, an awareness of the other person's concerns, and a sincere desire to understand the person.

What follows is a transcription of a conversation between a salesperson and customer. The salesperson is one of the top salespeople in the CE industry. He uses all of the techniques we have talked about. Try to identify them as they happen. Read on and listen to somebody else listening.

S: Hi.

C: Hi.

S: That's a pretty impressive looking camera. What kind is it?

C: A Hasselblad.

S: A Hasselblad?

C: Yes. It's a German camera that produces a larger negative than your conventional thirty-five millimeter cameras. It's most commonly used for protraits.

S: Sounds like a pretty special camera.

C: It is, but given what I shoot, I could use a thirty-five millimeter and get by. However, the larger format does give you a clearer picture.

S: What kind of photography do you do?

C: Mostly landscape.

S: Sounds like you're pretty serious about it.

C: I wish I had the time to get as serious as I would like to about it.

S: Where do you take pictures in this area?

C: Your typical tourist shots today. We're from Missouri.

S: Missouri?

C: Right, St. Louis.

S: That's beautiful country—so how long are you going to be here?

C: Not long enough, I'm afraid. We'll be going back Sunday, so I thought I would check out these compact disc players that I've been hearing so much about. You carry them, right?

S: We certainly do. What does your current system consist of?

C: It's a combination of things that I've put together over the years. Some KLH speakers, Dual turntable, and some older McIntosh stuff.

S: What kind of McIntosh stuff?

C: Integrated amp and tuner. It all still sounds pretty good.

S: I imagine it does. So you have an older but high quality system that sounds good, and now you're looking for the latest thing. There are a lot of advantages to compact disc players. What's the thing that appeals to you most about them?

C: Well, I've heard that you can listen to a whole record without changing sides and that the discs wear better than records. And given the fact that I used to have a reel-to-reel machine and liked it for similar reasons, I thought I would check out the compact disc thing.

S: Okay, so you're looking for increased playing time and a format that has better sound quality since it's more impervious to wear.

C: Right.

S: How large is your record collection?

C: I have a pretty extensive collection; in fact, every time I come down here, I leave a couple of hundred dollars lighter after visiting my favorite record store.

S: What store is that?

C: Village Music over in Marin County.

S: Oh, I know Village Music pretty well myself. It's a great record store. So about how many records would you say you have in total?

C: Pretty close to two thousand.

S: So you probably won't be converting to compact disc exclusively with that kind of investment in records. You said you have a Dual turntable—don't let me forget to ask you what kind of cartridge you're using. But first let me show you some of our compact disc players. Before giving you a demonstration, what else could I tell you about them?

C: Well, you're right. I'm not going to convert to compact disc completely, so I'm really not ready to invest a small fortune in the thing. What do they run?

S: You said a 'small fortune'?

C: Well, I heard you could get a decent player for under five hundred dollars. Is that right?

S: That's correct. Like so many other audio components, the cost depends upon the quality of sound and special features. And, of course, that's something that not only applies to audio . . . you were talking about the same thing when you were telling me about your camera.

And as with your camera—you don't always buy just as much quality as you need. Sometimes you buy *more* than you need, because of personal satisfaction or maybe because of an attitude that you have about buying precision equipment.

(Silence/smiling.)

C: The attitude part probably applies to me.

S: Let me show you a compact disc player that is a beautifully designed precision component and is very close to your price expectations. (The salesperson leads the customer into the room with the best speakers and before showing the customer a five hundred dollar CD player, asks what kind of cartridge the customer is currently using.)

Most salespeople think of listening as part of talking, and think that if they say the right things they will find out the right things about the customer.

As you can see, a lot of people have it backwards. Talking is something that we do to afford ourselves the opportunity to listen. Listening is the biggest part of communicating, and is the main thing you must do to get to know your customers and ensure your goal of mutual satisfaction.

STEP FIVE:
The Idea Is to Sell the Idea

The Idea Is to Sell the Idea

Selling the Right Idea

NOW THAT YOU'VE GATHERED enough information from your customers, you're ready to present the appropriate system or choice of components that will satisfy their needs. But the salesperson who merely presents the appropriate component to the customer won't achieve much success. Successful CE salespeople don't present products to their customers. They present ideas. That's because people don't really buy products. *They buy an idea of what the product will do for them.* The idea may take the form of a dream, fantasy, the first or final step of a plan, a personal need, or a simple pleasure. The product is just an accessory to these ideas. Your job is to find and then present the idea.

Think about going out right now and buying a new car. There're a lot of cars out there that will get you to the next off-ramp. They've all got seats, tires, an engine and a fair share of protective metal. So why do you have a favorite or a particular kind of car in mind? Because of the idea that the car represents. Maybe it's a Volvo and the main idea is safety. Maybe it's a Toyota and it's dependability. Or maybe it's a Ferrari and it's speed. The idea may also be status or good styling or good mileage, and, depending upon what you have now, any of these cars may fit the bill. As you can see, the idea that you as a customer are buying is not always just one-dimensional.

While the idea may have more than one aspect, there is usually one aspect that is more important than any other. Since in your line of business you are a salesperson and not an original manufacturer, you are sometimes going to have to present one aspect of the idea as being so grand that the customer feels it compensates for something else that may not be fully represented. If you do this well, you will be able to come close to fully satisfying not only the needs of your customer, but also the thing that they really came to buy—the idea.

What about buying a pair of loudspeakers? Almost any speaker you buy today, whether they're mini-satellites or studio monitors, will have an acceptable frequency response with minimal distortion and manage at least eighty dB SPL with one watt. They all make sound, don't they? But aside from the fact that they all act as efficient transducers—converting electrical energy into mechanical energy, thereby creating sound waves—they must play an even more important role and convert an idea into a reality.

Consider the idea of speakers. Different people have different ideas about speakers. Some people have the idea that speakers should look big and impressive and sound that way. Other people's idea of a speaker is that it should be as small as possible and surprise people with a big sound. And there are still other people who feel that speakers should be seen and not heard. Not a very exciting idea, but an idea still. Probably everybody has the idea that speakers should look good, but almost everybody's idea of a good looking speaker is different (finding that out is critical to the sale, and—as I've discussed in Step Four—the only way to find out is to listen to your customers before listening to the equipment).

If you were to ignore your customers' ideas about speakers or concentrate on only one aspect of their idea, you wouldn't sell very many speakers. The customer may tell you, "I'm looking for something that doesn't take up a whole lot of room but still puts out plenty of sound." If you show the customer a six-by-twelve foot wall of mylar and start telling him how he's going to get plenty of sound, you won't get very far. Your customer will probably give you a painful look and tell you that he just remembered he had a plane to catch. You addressed only one aspect of the idea—and it was the wrong one.

I have been shown wildly efficient speakers when I asked to see a well-balanced more neutral sounding speaker. And I have been shown a dubbing deck when I asked for a basic deck. I have been shown a receiver when I asked to see a tuner, changers when I asked for a simple turntable, and hi-bias tape when I asked for something to record lectures. At least, that's what I thought I had asked for, but evidently the fellow who was telling me about the mating habits of epitaxial particles didn't think that's what I meant. Finding out your customers' needs and then finding out their idea of the product, or expressing the idea of the product as it relates to them personally . . . that's the idea, but make sure you are on the right product. And don't fake it with a ringer, or pretend you didn't hear (the customer will believe you, and we know from Step Four who the salesperson that doesn't listen doesn't make the magic sell). It's a matter of finding the right idea, and selling it. When the customer buys the idea, the product goes with it.

Secret of a CE Legend

The salesperson who is adept at selling ideas does not compete with salespeople who sell equipment. There is no competition. It was my pleasure to know a CE salesperson who was legendary in the mid-seventies. He sold—out of the same location—over two-and-a-half-million dollars' worth of hi fi in four years. Some attributed his success to a broadcast-quality voice and an engaging personality. Others noted that he carried out equipment for his customers, and thought that might be one of the secrets of his success. As this was during the seventies; cowboy boots were fashionable footwear at that time, and since he wore them, other salespeople started wearing them. He also had a penchant for those little breath mint candies that rattled around in a little flip-top plastic container. And you soon noticed that several other salespeople were soon gulping down these noisy little mints.

But none of this mattered, of course, because he really

only did one thing: he followed all of the steps of the magic sell as a matter of course. He fully understood, "It's nice to be nice." Problems were not measured in dollars. Everyone, regardless of age, sex, or status, got the same preferential treatment. His greeting, which was a simple, "Hi," followed by a genuine smile, was so effective that other salespeople felt a sale was automatic with his next move. His next move was usually a question that gave him a chance to listen and to get to know the customer. And he listened like a psychologist who was being paid a hundred dollars an hour. He listened because he cared about each of his customers.

There was also something else that was noted by both the new and older salespeople in his store who had never taken the time to get beyond the faceplate or grill cloth of the equipment. He never talked about product, he never got *technical*; so they went one step further and concluded that this super star did not know product. They then decided that they didn't have to know product.

But this was where the salespeople's observations ended and where their presumptions (in their own defense) began. If you've been selling for a while, I'm sure you know that once the customer's needs are clarified and the careful process of presenting the right idea with the right products begins, the relationship between a salesperson and customer becomes more private, and is almost hidden from those who try to listen in or watch. (It's similar to what happens at a party. While the first drinks are being served, everybody listens to everybody and floats from one conversation to the next. But after the hors d'oeuvres are devoured, most people have found their partners and a passing remark by a passing loner can be an intrusion.) So based on what they couldn't hear, these salespeople assumed that their role model who had sold millions of dollars' worth of hi fi equipment wasn't that knowledgeable on product because he didn't appear to talk that much about it.

And he didn't. And nobody really knew how much he knew about all the equipment he had sold. When you don't know the depth of someone's knowledge on a given subject, however, it's risky business to presume ignorance. You might just be surprised and embarrassed at the same time. I was, when I coaxed him into a discussion on what was then one of the favorite topics of the industry—slewing rate limit. Now, this was a pretty complex technical subject, a subject that I hadn't yet grasped, but he had—or at least was trying to do his honest best to come to grips with it. I ended up listening to him for quite a while, and we eventually concluded that the marketing departments of the industry would someday tell us how worthwhile slewing rate would be as a specification.

But I learned that night that the number-one salesperson knew a lot more about produc than the number two's and three's would ever know, or that the customer would ever know, for that matter. The idea, he told me, was to, "Simply paint the picture for the customer." Something that they could relate to. Most customers related better to sound than slewing rate. It was the music that you wanted to present to the customer. "You help the customer," he said, "find their own private place and meaning in the music. And you used the hardware," he said, "to pick up reactions, glean the idea and sell." He kept the specs reserved for the person who needed them. He calculated that the knowledgeable customer—the person who needed the numbers and schematics—accounted for about seventeen percent of his total business. So at once he made a good case for sticking with the idea of it all, painting a picture that included rather than excluded the customer, and also knowing about the gear for more reasons than confidence-building and credibility-signals. . . . Seventeen percent of two-and-a-half million dollars' worth of sales is $425,000.00. That's a pretty good reason for getting to know the product.

How to Make a Feature Worthwhile

Knowing the function of all features, and having some technical understanding about every component, is the only way you can sell the main idea of any product. But if you miss the idea, you'll miss the "magic sell."

Allow me to recount a recent shopping excursion of my own.

I've just entered a store which will remain nameless and,

for the deserted salesperson than for myself. I can always find another salesperson. But what about the salesperson? Chances are that it might be a couple of days before another customer walks in prepared to spend fifteen hundred dollars on a car stereo—which was the amount of money that I had alloted for something that I had finally decided to buy, and, as they say, do it right.

And I would have, had the salesperson done it right. I was looking for the magic sell, and was determined not to buy until I found it. I wanted a good car stereo system bad. I had done more than my share of research, which was fortunate, as I found out on more than just this one occasion. I've had salepeople feed me features as if they were passing out free samples of cheesespread in a supermarket. A taste of the feature and I was supposed to nod or shake my head and tell the salesperson whether I liked it. No further explanation necessary.

When somebody says, "Modulated power supply," that's what I hear, not much more. (Having spent a number of years in the industry, I tend to do some translation of these terms which you wouldn't expect from the layman, so let's leave me in the middle of my dilemma for a little while and think in terms of the average car stereo buyer. Later I'll tell you about what I bought and why I finally decided to buy it.)

Harry the salesperson had been friendly enough, and was neatly attired. He had even asked a couple of questions before launching into his every-feature-is-famous spiel. But the features that began popping out of his mouth seemed to have nothing to do with the questions that he had asked the customer . . . why? Because he didn't explain the features, or even ask if an explanation would be helpful before pointing to another one. He didn't give the customer an idea of what the feature did or how it would personally benefit the customer. Whatever he found out about the customer's needs was—to the customer—useless information because the customer didn't know what Harry was talking about most of the time. The customer's idea of what he wanted was unimportant since the customer didn't get an idea of what these features did. (And if you don't know what a feature does, it's really not a feature is it?)

You've probably heard about features and benefits . . . the benefit is why the feature exists. The benefit is the idea behind the feature that can make an item personally useful or enjoyable to the user. A coffee cup has a handle. The handle allows you to get a better grip on the cup without burning your hand. That's a benefit. That's the idea of the handle. If I had never seen a coffee cup before and you said, "This cup has a nice handle," and didn't explain further, I might think that the main reason for the handle was to hang the cup on a hook or a device to keep the cup from rolling off the table when you lay it on its side, or maybe just a decorative ornament, and later burn my fingers upon discovering that none of these things were the main benefit. It probably wouldn't take too long for me to understand the benefit—the idea of the feature called a handle.

But I could go a lifetime without getting the idea of 70- or 120-*us* equalization, a music sensor, or a modulated power supply. And thanks to Harry and company, a lot of people have. That's too bad, since those are things the customers paid for, and then never know whether they're using them or not. Even if they are, they don't perceive the advantage or the benefit—they don't get the idea. "What they don't know won't hurt them or help them," is the rationale of salespeople who are looking out for their own immediate best interests at the expense of customers and future business.

Nor would it do much good to merely explain what 70- or 120-*us* equalization does. "Sometimes an audio signal of flat frequency response tends to drop off at the extreme high and low ends. An equalization is a special circuit that compensates for this, raising the low and high parts of the frequency response curves." Wonderful. So what does that mean to the customer? "Better signal-to-noise ratio." And what does that mean? "The ratio of voltage between the loudest undistorted tone that you hear and the noise and hum when the signal is reduced to zero." That makes a lotta sense . . . to someone, but certainly not to a person who did not know what equalization was good for. The person who doesn't need the explanation, in no more time than it takes to safely navigate a turnstile and say, "Looking for a nice car stereo," I find myself standing in front of a car stereo display and a salesperson who is pointing to a unit that's at eye level and has about sixteen buttons all with numbers or multi-directional arrows.

"This cassette tuner has Dolby B and Dolby C," he says, "and also has a circuit to correct high frequency errors before Dolby decoding. It's also autoreverse, equipped with a music sensor, has motor-assisted loading, switchable 70 or 120 us equalization, and has a quartz-Pll tuner with six FM and six AM presets, auto-scan tuning, and—what I really like—is this switch here that automatically selects the tuner while a tape is fast-winding. What do you think? Pretty nifty, huh?"

I think I'm already confused and tired, and I've just gotten started. In a vain attempt to re-orient myself, and gain back my self-respect as an educated consumer, I say, "You said this is a cassette tuner, which I assume means. . . ."

"You're pretty quick on the draw," he interrupts me. "It means just what you think it means. It *means* that you're gonna need an amp, but don't worry, we've got a couple that are state of the art. Modulated power supplies, four channel, the works—you just name it, and we have it."

"And of course I'm also going to need. . . ."

"Speakers! And we have some speakers that you won't believe. What kinda car do you have?"

"Alfa Romeo."

"Oh that's some kinda car. Wouldn't wantta sell it would yuh? No, just kiddin'. So you're gonna have one sweet little Italian music box. My name's Harry by the way, what's yours?"

"Stan. And I was wondering if I. . . ."

"Needed an equalizer, right? Well now that's up to you but do you. . . ."

"Have a card?" I ask with what I think is exquisite timing.

"A what? A card? Well Stan I have a card, but you know you can't listen to a card like. . . ."

"I wasn't planning on listening to it," I explain. And trying not to be too abrupt, I tell him I gotta go. I feel sorrier however, would understand what you're talking about. Ironic isn't it? The people who understand don't need it, and the people who need it don't understand.

It would probably be a pretty good idea to concentrate on the idea of equalization. "It means that you're going to hear cleaner, crisper highs and deeper, richer bass. (Remember that line?) It means that you have the ability to fine-tune the tape deck to any kind of tape you use. You will have the ability to get optimum sound from all of your recordings. More music and less tape noise, which is especially important in your case, since you have a convertible and will often be playing the stereo louder to compensate for wind and traffic noise. It's also important because you said you were a musician and since you have a trained ear, you are able to detect subtle differences that escape other people's ears. It's a feature that's especially important to you." Now, the customer might buy the deck especially because of that feature. You get the idea across. And the idea seemed custom made for that customer's special needs. But remember, you could not have given the customer the main idea unless you had known the information that the customer didn't understand; your technical understanding will allow you to give un-technical explanations that make good sense.

Remember the advice of a legend: "Paint a picture that includes rather than excludes the customer." And, "You help the customer find their own private place and meaning in the music."

The Background for the Idea

Consider the feature before it got to *you*, the CE salesperson. After somebody designed a feature, you can bet that somebody said, "That's a good idea," or it would never have made it past the drawing board. And somebody thought it was a good idea because somebody else explained the idea of the feature—advantages, benefits, things like that. Now, doesn't it make sense that the person who the feature was designed for—the customer—should be privy to the same kind of explanation?

It not only makes sense, but it is the only way to sell the idea. And remember that's what people buy—or, to be more exact, that's what people buy when they feel good about buying. *The satisfied customer gets the idea.* When you say, "Modulated power supply," that's all the customer hears. The customer does not hear, "That's a smaller and more efficient amplifier design that allows the manufacturer to offer you more power for less money. The voltage stays low, just like your car idling, for music that doesn't demand much power, but rises, like an extremely fast-accelerating car, for passages of music that demand peak power." (*Now the most important part—matching the idea of this particular amp to the customer's main idea of a car stereo...*) "And since you're thinking of putting a fifteen-inch woofer in the trunk, and want people to hear you coming before they see you, you should probably take a look at an amplifier with a modulated power supply."

If you say, "Modulated power supply," and leave it at that, then you have a feature without a home. The customer doesn't hear your explanation about peak-power needs, even though you might be thinking it and are able to deliver it—and therefore the customer doesn't really have any reason to need it, want it, or take it home unless you're throwing it in for free.

Remember, customers will take any feature you mention if it doesn't cost anything. But, as an example, if you expect the customer to spend four or five hundred dollars for a cassette tuner that can't even move a tweeter and requires the customer to spend another four or five hundred dollars for an amplifier and speakers, you had better be prepared to:

1) SCAN THE INFORMATION you got from the customer when you were listening to him describe his needs, and....

2) KEY IN ON THE FEATURES at your disposal, and give him an idea of how they will personally benefit him, and....

3) PAINT A PICTURE with the help of the presentation techniques that I'll be discussing, and you will have

him doing something that he might have only dreamed about before he came to see you.

Harry was telling the customer about a circuit that corrected high frequency errors before Dolby decoding, and he didn't really know whether the customer knew what Dolby did, let alone Dolby B and C. If the customer had said he liked to listen to classical music and female vocals and had a super cassette deck at home, Harry could have made a very good case for the customer owning a cassette tuner with that degree of NR sophistication. But that also entails knowing more about the feature than its trademark or patented name. It's a simple matter of knowing what you're talking about. Whether you're selling VCR's or boats, it's important to know what you're talking about. How would you like to go shopping for your first boat with a salesperson who didn't know a motor sailer from a Boston whaler, or the advantage that one might have over the other?

Is it much different not knowing the difference between VHS, Beta, and 8mm? The sum total of dollars changing hands might be significantly larger in one case, but in both cases the significance of the ignorance poses an equally dismal threat to customer satisfaction.

When considering the importance of product knowledge, make a careful distinction between knowing what you're talking about and knowing when to talk about it. You may not need a nautical history or care about who designed the first Boston whaler, but you would be comfortable knowing that your salesperson had that kind of background to call upon if you needed it. The same applies to you as the salesperson. The customer probably does not care about hearing about the difference between Omega and M-wrap tape mechanisms, but would certainly be comfortable knowing that you knew about such things—and, in fact, *expects* you to know about that and more. He might want to know about 8mm, and this other thing they've heard about—digital audio tape. What do you know about that?

The buyer came to a CE store or department because he or she wanted more background, assistance, and information about their purchase than they could get from a catalogue. How much you give them depends upon what you find out about them and their needs in the listening process. No standard dosage or minimum daily requirement of product information and technical knowledge has ever been established for the CE customer. We all have different needs relative to different things.

Understanding and getting to know the products you carry is at once the easy and difficult part. It's easy because all it takes is a couple of magazine subscriptions, some conversation with people who make it their business and their pastime to know almost everything there is to know, and some hands-on experience with the multi-featured wonder machines that outfit the environment where you spend a big part of your life.

It's only difficult because it means making the effort to learn. There may be a magic sell, but there is no magic pill. It means taking time to listen to people who know more than you do, and reading owner's manuals before the prospective owner arrives on the scene and asks you what "auto-scan" does. It means researching and playing with the gear until you can operate it as though you owned it. What you have to do to become knowledgeable is what most people would call fun. Don't take the fun and excitement of your job for granted. Just because you're getting paid for it, doesn't mean it has to be work.

Techniques of Painting the Picture

When you have an idea of what the customer expects from a chosen component or system, it is your turn to paint the picture—to present the right idea in the light of your expertise so that it complements the customer. And the component becomes more than just another piece of equipment. There is no baby spot shining on the component that you are presenting to your customer. Take a turntable for an example, which is sitting somewhere in a display that hold dozens of other similarly shaped objects with black platters and plexiglass dustcovers. If the turntable you're focusing on is going to look like something special—so special and uniquely right for him that the customer is going to say "I'll take it, today!"—it's going to take all the ingenuity and sensibility you have. You have daily intimate contact with hundreds of home-entertainment products and, if you're adequately prepared, you know them on a first name and hands-on basis—by price, brand, model number, and feature. Right?

It's amazing to think about the Britannica-sized bulk of knowledge and information which you would appear to have regarding the equipment you sell. Almost every audio/video store or department carries several products of at least forty or fifty different manufacturers. Larger consumer electronics stores and superstores may handle products of hundreds of manufacturers. But if I do a very conservative calculation, and assume that you carry four products of each manufac-turer (and in most cases you carry many more than that) then apparently you know the features, functions and cost of 160 to 200 products. Is that true? Many of you can answer yes. Some of you will say, "I guess so." Others will say, "I don't think so." And another person might say, "It really doesn't matter." Your answer generally depends upon how long you've been in the business of selling home entertainment equipment. Your answer may also depend upon your perspec-tive of the presentation, and what you think it takes to paint the perfect picture. Because you see, the person who said, "It really doesn't matter," was right. Let me explain what he meant.

Remember, I said, "...the knowledge and information you would *appear* to have," and, later, "...*apparently* you know the features, functions and cost of 160 to 200 prod-ucts." *Apparently* is just what I meant, and not *actually*. Successful CE salespeople know that there are techniques which serve well as a substitute for a photographic memory. They know that many products share the same features, and also that many features that have different names and trade-marks perform the same functions. They are also able to come within plus-or-minus twenty dollars of the cost of an item after a good one-minute appraisal of a component and its features. They might have to press a few buttons or ask what this new feature does before giving their guesstimate, but give them a minute and they'll be in the ballpark.

So you see, the person who said, "It really doesn't matter if I know the features, functions and cost of two hundred components," was right, and would go on to say, "but it *does* matter that I know the features, functions, and cost of representative components in each category and price range." It matters so much that without this overall perspective—versus a feat of memory—the salesperson wouldn't be able to perform a far more important function for the customer than that performed by any one feature. . . . Presenting the idea. Even though you know the similarity between different models as well as the importance of new features, it is your ingenuity and ability to make a product special for a special person, to paint a picture that has personal meaning . . . and makes enough of a difference to make the sale. Your customers can find the details of each individual product in catalogues, product guides and directories, and also in the owner's manual that comes free of charge with each piece of equipment. Your knowledge though, is ultimately more sophisticated than that of an owner's manual, and your service doesn't come free. Since the customers are paying for your service, let's make sure they get their money's worth—*more* than their money's worth, so they'll make a point of doing business with you again.

Let me provide a word of caution about techniques of presentation. There is no pat scenario for each product. Can you imagine carrying around approximately a dozen canned scenarios—one for each component category? Boring—real boring! That's the job of the vegimatic salesman, not the CE salesperson.

As you review the methods which follow, remember that they apply to different people in different situations. Knowing when to use any particular one is determined by your ability to listen to the customer, discover his needs, glean the idea, paint the picture, watch for reactions, and present the idea until it is unequivocally saleable.

ANALOGY: Letting the customer relate to something that *you* are familiar with by comparing it to something that *he* is familiar with. You know the customer drives a

THE IDEA IS TO SELL THE IDEA 109

sports car. Compare a brand new stylus shape's ability to track a record groove to the ability of the car's radial tires to stick to the pavement in tight curves, where it counts. Or, the customers are debating between buying a full-featured receiver or separate components. The man has a cast on his leg. Tell them how the separates are more specialized in their functions, how each component is dedicated to doing one thing particularly well. Mention to the customer that a general practitioner probably could have set his broken leg, but he was no doubt happy to have the specialized services of an orthopedist.

ANECDOTES: Making an observation about the customer, or relating a brief personal experience that will have the customer recognizing the importance of his or her purchase. The customer is well-dressed, and obviously cares about her self-appearance. She just wanted a basic Walkman for jogging, but saw a bright red AM/FM autoreverse stereo cassette recorder with Dolby noise reduction, and doesn't know whether she should splurge. You motion to her purse and tell her that that doesn't look like your basic purse, but it's very handsome and will probably be something that she will enjoy using for a much longer time than your basic bag. Or, in the same instance, "That reminds me...." pointing to your own shoes.... "of the time I bought these shoes. These loafers are the first pair of Italian shoes I've had. I used to think that the thrill of buying them was the best thing about them, and now, a year later, given how they look and how I feel about them, I realize I bought something that I really could afford even though I didn't think it at the time. A basic Walkman might be fine for somebody else, but I just don't think it's your style." The salesperson also used the technique of complimenting the customer—something that we have talked about all along. And when you build the self-esteem of someone else, you feel better about yourself. (But remember, you've got to mean it or you'll come off as a phony.)

ENDORSEMENTS: Use yourself, or another expert, or a famous personality, or a magazine equipment review or consumer report recommendation or another satisfied customer as testimony and validation of the quality or reliability of the product that the customer is interested in. "If I didn't own a couple already, that would certainly be the Walkman I'd buy. Plus, red is one of my two favorite colors. What about you?" Or, to a rock fan, "That must be a pretty good set of headphones. One of the sound people from Dire Straits was in last week and bought that identical set for Mark Knopfler. You must really know your equipment." Or, to a classics buff, "You might find it interesting that a recent article about music systems of famous musicians said that those are the speakers that Sejii Ozawa owns. You'll certainly be in good company." Or, to a person who says that the last tape deck he bought was the one recommended by his friend who knows all there is to know about this stuff, you might want to ask the store manager to come over and give his expert opinion on the new tape deck, and bolster your recommendation as well as enhance the credibility of the product being considered by the customer. Two recommendations are better than one, unless one is famous.

PREDICTION AND PROOF: *One of the most effective techniques of presenting*: a statement regarding quality of sound or picture, or the feel of quality craftmanship or precision engineering is not of much use unless the customer believes you. You know what they say about seeing is believing—the same thing holds true for hearing and feeling. Tell the customer what kind of picture, type of sound, or ease of operation that he is going to see, hear or feel, and then prove it by playing it for him or letting him push the right button. This technique is obviously useful in the demonstration of speakers. Rather than just telling the customer that speaker A is going to sound better than speaker B, tell him why A will sound better than B and what to listen for so he can prove it to himself.

This, of course, means that you must be familiar with the sound characteristics of the speakers that you sell, the relative picture quality of TV's and monitors, and must know your software, whether it's CD, LP, cassette, VHS, Beta, 8mm, or videodisc. And also know the cut, section or band which will prove everything you said to be absolutely true. If the customers don't let you know they can see or hear or feel the difference, repeat the demonstration with the same tape, but not before pointing out something additional that they should be listening to or looking for. "Okay, when the the Imperial star destroyer comes into the picture, look at the sky and the stars. Notice how black the sky is on set A, and how white the stars are. The blacker the better. And look to see on which set the twinkling—or the light of the stars— is most visible. Okay, let's watch that scene again, ready?"

Or use a different tape if the customer is not that excited with the demo material you chose. But never forget to explain what he's going to see or hear or feel before hitting the ON button. The software needs your help if it's going to make a dynamic enough impression to sell the hardware. And wait for the customer's reaction to make sure that he's experienced what you said he would.

When a person experiences something positive that you told him about, he is going to want to experience it again and again—in the privacy of his own home—and every time he does, he'll remember who was there to share it with him the first time. Being remembered as part of a positive experience is the biggest part of your job.

DEFINITION OF TERMS: This is more of a guideline than a technique. When you introduce a feature by its real name, make sure the customers know why it's there. Tell them what it does: "And it has an anti-rolling transport," you say, looking at a couple of blank expressions, "which means that you're not going to detect a deviation in the speed of the tape when you're running, so you'll hear smooth play every stride of the way.'' Their blank expressions have turned to smiles upon hearing what now sounds like a good idea. An idea worth buying.

Use the above techniques at the right time with the right person—keeping in mind his or her unique needs—and you will have painted a picture of a product worth owning. In the next section, I'll give you an example of a salesperson who did just that.

The Best Feature Is the Idea

Knowing what to talk about and when to do it depends on what you have found out about your customer. But as I said, there are no pat explanations of benefits—and there is no encyclopedia of ideas. There are feature directories which tell you what a feature does—but that's only half of it. *The feature is the idea. The idea is the only thing that makes the feature worthwhile. The idea is what the feature does for the unique needs of each customer.* And as we talked about, a good idea can get better if you apply your personal experience and imagination to the feature as it relates to a particular person. You do this by making frequent use of personal anecdotes, or analogies.

Everything can always be compared to something else which the customer is more familiar with and closer to than the equipment. It's like saying, ''Here, take a clearer look at it through the binoculars.'' That's when a whatchamacallit becomes worth buying. If the customer whom Harry was talking to had said that he listened to tapes in his car but mainly listened to FM to preview selections from records that he might want to buy, then Harry could have made a good case for a quartz-Pll tuner, presets, and auto-scan tuning—but Harry didn't. And I was the customer who said just that.

On the following day, a salesperson who heard me say it, didn't treat it as idle chatter. She asked me what were the things that irritated me the most about listening to FM in the car. It was a question that I was eager to answer. After I had described everything from drifting stations to the stress-inducing effects of static, she focused on the accuracy of the tuner, the clarity of sound, and the convenience of stereo when I wanted it rather than when the lay of the land allowed it. She asked what stations I usually listened to, and encouraged me to tune in to a couple of them and—and even though the reception wasn't bad—she assured me that reception would be even better in my car. She even gave me an estimate of the range for effective stereo reception before the stereo blend circuit would come to my aid. And I agreed with her— I'd rather listen to half stereo without static rather than stereo I couldn't bear.

She made sure that I bought a unit with a digital tuner with presets that would stay preset rather than play surprises on me—and she said it had enough presets so that my wife and children could also preset their favorite stations. That was a good idea, I agreed. Nobody would have to endure another person's musical taste for any longer than it took to press a button. And the buttons were so sensitive that they were a pleasure to push, she pointed out, rather than feeling as though you were pushing a circuit breaker. And, as an aside, she reminded me that there would be times that I would be listening to tapes, and rather than listening to the reel and rattle of a cassette rewind, the tuner would automatically come on. Given how much I liked FM, she went on, I might just choose to continue listening to the radio. Music should be a pleasure to play as well as listen to, she told me.

Before leaving the store, I had felt the touch of sensitive switches and heard static-free FM, and I was already thinking about how much more pleasurable the drive to and from from the office would be. She personally recommended an installer who guaranteed his work, and who also carried a special antenna that I might want to consider for even better reception. I ended up buying a case of tape, because she reminded me that I would be doing more taping now than before—not because I would necessarily be listening to more tapes in the car, but *because* (and such was her keen awareness of my needs) I would probably be buying more records now that I was hearing better FM more often—and therefore doing even more taping for my sister-and-brother-in-law whom I had told her about, and who lived in an area that was far from record stores or FM stations. I also asked her about what was new in cartridges, which I shouldn't have, because she suggested one that I'll soon find a way to afford.

Harry had memorized a list of features, but the salesperson I bought my car stereo system from (and in turn told you about), remembered my needs and spoke to those needs with *me* personally in mind. She skillfully used all of the presentation techniques that I have talked about. I knew I needed each feature that she pointed out, because I knew what it did for me. I heard the sound of the speakers I bought . . . an "autotorium" version of my home system, she quipped.

While in the store I set the presets to two of my favorite stations—and it was as easy as she had predicted. I knew the system that she sold me was top-rated—all of the components had been given laudatory reviews by two consumer CE publications which I subscribe to. She said it was a pleasure to talk with someone who knew the equipment, and who had a keen ear—compliments which I accepted painlessly. She asked what kind of home system I had, and when I told her, she said that she would like to own the equivalent some day. I said that shouldn't be too long if she just kept doing what she was doing. But why—she was curious—did I have a tape deck if I didn't listen to tapes all that often? I didn't feel that the question was too personal at all. In fact, I was delighted to tell her about my sister and brother-in-law who had recently given up the city for life in the country—and I noticed that I was carrying out an additional box because of that little anecdote.

But I felt good about it. Finally I wouldn't have to scurry through desk drawers and book cases looking for a blank tape or one that I could record over every time I bought an album that I wanted to record for them. There was something else that she said right before I left and which I repeated as soon as I got home. "I sold almost this identical system to another fellow," she said. "He had a nice Italian car, too. It was a Ferrari. A Dino? Is that something like yours?" As much as she would like to have a system like mine some day, I would like to own a Dino some day. "Yes," I replied. "It's something like mine."

Her idea of a good car stereo was worth buying. And she

made me feel as if the store was a fun place that had been especially equipped for my needs, rather than a technical trap that I was going to have to find my way out of. I felt the logic of a good conversation happening as she highlighted the idea of the features that were worth her time and my time. There was sequence and order to her presentation, just as there had been when she had asked me questions about what I wanted and why I felt I needed them. I never felt that I was about to be ambushed by some cute comment; instead, I felt that someone was listening who had my best interests in mind.

On the other hand, I felt that Harry could have been replaced by a digital readout similar to the one on the tuner that I bought. And I'm sure that he felt that he was a very efficient salesperson trying hard to be an expert, but he expressed himself like an auctioneer peddler and came across about as personal as the latest product directory.

The magic sell is definitely efficient, but it is far more than that—it's understanding the customer. Harry's approach was definitely quantity over quality, probably because he had never bothered to learn about things like the silent question, the way-to-go approach, selling the idea, or listening as applied to selling. Selling has too often been misinterpreted as something you do to or don't do for someone. Something I mentioned earlier . . . what they don't know won't hurt them or help them—or—another technique belonging to the offspring of Willy Loman: if you talk enough about enough things, the customer will be impressed enough to buy whatever it is whether he needs it or not. Harry was trying hard to do a lot of things for himself, but not letting me, the customer, do anything—including buying something . . . even when I had a pretty good idea of what I wanted. As a customer, I was just looking for someone to personalize that idea so I could enjoy myself more.

Harry should take all of the features that he listed and make an effort to find out how they personally benefit different people with different needs, and then use those features to focus his presentation. Customers find the idea of buying something in a CE store pretty intriguing. The salesperson's presentation should make that idea even more interesting and exciting—not less so.

In the CE store, you never have to feature a feature that nobody came to see, because there's always something new for everybody, even me.

* * *

When you like what you're selling—let's take speakers for an example since that's what we started out talking about—you feel that a speaker is more than a highly-engineered box. You'll find yourself communicating the sense and excitement of that box until your customer is thinking about everything except woofers, tweeters and crossovers. That's when your customer reaches for his wallet and asks whether you want him to pay cash or credit. It's your ability to present an enticing image that makes the customer reach. The speaker boxes that the customer loads into his car are bigger than a dishwasher and two micro-waves put together or smaller than a loaf of bread, but they contain something far more important than loudspeakers.

Loudspeakers are made of particle board and veneer, polypropylene, magnets, capacitors, fuses, and things like that. But these boxes contain sound that can reach into the solar plexus and send you reeling; music which can wring tears and have you laughing the next moment, riffs and rhythms that get you up and won't let you down, and melodies that transcend walls and ceilings and the normal boundaries of a room. A room that is now saturated and bathed in the wonderful decibles of a daring good idea. That's what's in those boxes, and never forget it. The boxes make the idea a reality, but without the idea and everything that it communicates, there wouldn't be that much to get excited about, would there?

STEP SIX:
Answering the Question of Price

The Cheap Question You Don't Have to Ask

DESPITE ALL YOUR PREPARATION, your practiced opening and insightful questions, you will occasionally run into customers who want to talk more about what they expect than what they really want. They don't seem interested in either communicating or getting down to business. They're everywhere and nowhere at the same time. Maybe they're being purposefully vague because they're intimidated by the store, or maybe they're suspicious of salespeople in general, or maybe they're just excited. It doesn't really matter, because the situation is salvageable, and the magic sell is still yours to make if you continue using the techniques you've learned and don't resort to "the cheap question." Let me give you an example.

Two young guys swagger into the store looking for the best system in town, and it appears that they just started thinking about it a couple of seconds before screeching to a halt in front of your door. They want speakers with a lotta bass, "Big speakers like Tony has," but they don't know what kind of speakers Tony has, and furthermore, they don't want to take the time to think about it because they've got "Things to do and places to go," and besides, they want a dubbing deck, too, so they can start making tapes for their friends, and they've got a lotta friends, and they want plenty of power too, because "How else you gonna get a lotta bass?" and they want a CD player, too, because "It's the newest thing, right?" And so they want the newest thing. "Obviously!" And they want to, "See the stuff and not just talk about it, you know what I mean?" They want to see it all at once, evidently because one guy is already off looking at tape decks while the other guy, who you're now following, is heading for a pair of thousand dollar speakers.

"Hey Joe," his friend calls from across the store. "Come over here! Look at this thing, will yuh?" You look over before Joe does, and notice that his buddy is looking at a four-hundred dollar dubbing deck. When they regroup, you want to stop the rambling, gain some focus, and just get down to business. You ask the main man the bottom-line question. The cheap question. "How much," you ask, "do you guy's want to spend?" And you get a unexpected reply, but an appropriate one—"What'sa matter man, don't you think we have any money?" It turns out this isn't the first place they've been to, even though that's the way it may have appeared. They've been asked that question before by lesser salespeople than you. And don't assume that they have a chip on their shoulder, because if they do, so do I. In your haste to pin them down, you just put them uptight. By taking a short cut, you might have just cut yourself out of some good business.

"How much do you want to spend?" When a salesperson asks me that question, I'm insulted. And whether I'm looking at a mountain bike or a Walkman, I'll usually reply with something like, "I'd like to spend about two dollars, tops. Why would I *like* to spend more?" I grant you that there are words in that dialogue, but there sure isn't much communication to speak of, because the salesperson has just proven to me that he is either more interested in my money than in me, or he doesn't know his product and he's trying to get around it by asking an irrelevant, presumptuous question. Whatever his reason, he hasn't inspired any trust, and trust is what you're going to need to be successful and build your fair share of repeat business.

Asking that question doesn't help put your customers at ease; it challenges them. It puts them on the spot. It flusters them. Just when the customers had stopped thinking about money upon entering the store and getting a dazzling view of the real thing—all the components and systems that they've thought about now right before their eyes—somebody decides to do a reality check and ask how much money they were going spend. Now, instead of the customers communicating their needs and desires, however disorganized, and talking about big bass and fancy dubbing decks, you've just drawn the line—the bottom line—and the language is dollars. In effect, the salesperson has said, "Put your money where your mouth is." And it's hard to do that and communicate at the same time.

The language of dollars is also a hard language for many of your customers to speak. Maybe they haven't been in a audio/video store in a few years, and they were planning on having you show them what they could get with the amount they budgeted for themselves to spend, and in the process, making up their minds whether they should spend more or less. But now they don't have that option, so they spit out their budgeted number. "Around five hundred," they say, looking at you anxiously to see if they should blush or smile. You can feel the awkwardness of this customer situation as much as they can, and in a move to get it over with, you reply with something like, "Great. Let me show you what I have." (Just listen to those words for a moment: "Let *me* show *you* what *I* have." Does it sound as if you're about to do something *to* or *with* the customer? Mutual understanding doesn't seem too much in the offing here.) So without much mutual feeling of any kind, you show the customers a five hundred dollar rack system, and they say, "Okay, thanks. Why don't you give us your card 'cause we got some other places we want to check out, too." They just said, "Thanks but no thanks," and you just wasted another card.

This question—which is responsible for destroying more relationships than any question ever asked in retail—is often used as a crutch when you start showing the equipment. It can happen when you come to a component that you don't sell that much, or that you really haven't acquainted yourself with.

"You're right, it's a very advanced unit," you tell the married couple who you've been showing an audio system to. "It has all the features that you'll need for full audio and video compatibility, and more than enough power to accommodate the dynamic range of Compact disc, especially at the volume levels at which you like to occasionally play your music, and this...this is the new equalizer that...." *That,* you are pointing to, but are totally unfamiliar with, so in lieu of highlighting a feature, you say, "How much were you people planning on spending?" You ask the question as if it were suddenly a crucial point, even though you chose to present the system you're standing in front of for good reasons based on good information.

The people who were just starting to feel that they were getting personal treatment, now look at each other and with wrinkling foreheads, say, "I don't know, a thousand or so." You say, "Oh great, then what we're looking at is right in your price range," speeding past the equalizer to the dubbing deck, which you will paint a beautiful picture around and which had better be magnificent...because you almost have to go back to step one.

Any good feeling that you have established up to this point has been shaken by suspicion. The price question does several things *to* the customers:

1. They question their own appearance, or status. They wonder if you are asking, "How much?" because it's suddenly occurred to you that they might not be able to afford it and you might be wasting your time.

2. They question your motives or reasons for doing what you are doing. Obviously, they know you're not working for free, but somehow they fooled themselves into thinking that you were more concerned about getting the right equipment for them rather than the right price or commission for yourself.

3. Their primary concern is getting the right equipment, and two or three hundred dollars one way or the other really isn't their primary concern. But suddenly the husband remembers his neighbor George talking about how you could get a good discount on all this stuff, and the husband whispers to his wife, "Don't get too excited, because we might just want to do some looking around." In any case, they are now not going to buy the system for the price that it's marked at.

As I said, the dubbing deck better come off looking bigger than life, because you have just thrown a major obstacle in your own path by resorting to a cheap question rather than making an honest statement that would have solved your problem and made you you look even more credible.

As we talked about in the last chapter, you'll never be surprised or at a loss for words over a new product if you have a good generic definition of the function of the main features of components in each product category. Maybe the equalizer has buttons rather than sliders, or more bands than you've ever worked with, but you still know the main function and features of an equalizer, and you can talk briefly about the advantages of "The most sophisticated tone control" in the store. And if they want to know more about this specific model, say: "That's a brand-new model that I haven't had a chance to put on the test-bench yet, but let me show you the dubbing deck which you asked about, and then I can get the owner's manual and we can review the features of this new equalizer together."

The chances are slim that they will take you up on this offer. They will probably be more interested in figuring out how to hook it all up and where to put the system than taking the time now to investigate the features of a component that they feel is the newest and most advanced thing in the store. You'll be glad to make good on your offer, however, and they believe that—and that degree of honesty and your offer to help is almost better than an expert review of the component.

Now let's go back to the first situation with the two young guys who wanted it all right now. By using a more regulated form of active listening and by using details in your reflective statement that are important to the customer, you'll be able to effectively focus the attention of the customers in this instance. The conversation will sound something like:

S: You're looking for system with a dubbing deck, right?

C: Right, but we've seen some really fantastic out-of-sight machines and we don't just want any old dubbing deck, if you know what I mean.

S: So you're looking for something *special* in a

dubbing deck and I also remember you wanted speakers that will play loud, really loud, without making funny cracking sounds, and you want a lot of good deep bass, so it's just like hearing ZZ Top live at the Rosemont Horizon, right?

C: You got it, so when do we listen to all this stuff?

S: Right now. But first I've got to tell you guys about a couple of very important features that most people don't even know about yet. Then I want to go in that sound room over there and give you guys a demonstration you won't forget, okay?

You can be assured that it'll be okay. By being very specific with your reflective questions, but using a few broad brush strokes and painting the picture with the details they gave you, you have your customers feeling as if they're doing the talking when actually all they're doing is nodding and affirming what they told you—except now *you're* saying it. They're not saying much more than they were before, but they're participating. And they feel as though they have been heard rather than shut down. You may be repeating what they have told you, but you've said it just as they imagined it—and it sounds even better than they imagined, since it's coming from someone else—so their level of anticipation is boosted a couple of notches and they switch to an active mode rather than just musing or being amusing. They want to listen, and they start feeling the urge to buy from someone who understands them, rather than an urge to leave and play this easy-come-easy-go game with someone else who will ask them the same cheap question that discounts their value as customers and, if they do stick around, will soon have you discounting the equipment.

Treat every customer as someone who is seriously concerned about making a purchase. That means you should uphold the value of the things they came to buy, rather than acting as if you're their accountant. When you ask price in an attempt to focus your presentation, you have taken the focus off the equipment and put it back on the ads they read before coming to the store. The result is that you've got them shopping again rather than buying. Neither you nor the customer have made any progress by making a special point of asking, "How much do you want to spend?"

Most people don't know any more about the price of audio/video equipment than they know about the price of property. The average person knows that a piece of property with an ocean view or on a hilltop, costs more than a tract parcel, but there are so many variables, that estimating land value takes an expert. The average person also knows that bigger speakers usually cost more than smaller speakers, and that more watts usually cost more than fewer watts, but beyond that, an expert is needed. And you're the expert.

Aside from the factor of the customers' ignorance for which they are not to be blamed, when you ask a person how much he wants to spend, you are, in effect, saying, "Let me see your wallet, and then I'll show you the gear." Again, put yourself in the customer's place. Is that one of the first two or three things that you would like to be asked when you enter a store that doesn't have a price tag on every item? Wouldn't you rather have somebody say something about you, and ask about what you need, rather than immediately being subjected to a credit check? After you buy something, even personal friends will be discreet about asking the price of something. "Do you mind if I ask how much it cost?" Or, "I don't mean to pry, but could you tell me how much you'd have to pay for something like that?"

Have you heard questions like that? The friend or acquaintance is asking your permission to ask what they consider a personal question, but believe it or not, there are hundreds of salespeople poised at this very moment ready to ask you first thing: "How much do you want to spend?" As a salesperson, you have the right to get personal, but with a sense of discretion.

You can also predict one of two responses to the cheap question. 1: If the customer has some idea of how much he wants to spend (*want*, not *will*, spend), he will give you the minimum without stretching it. This means that after the customers tell you, "Five hundred," you will feel obliged to build in the stretch and take them to something costing six hundred, as if you never really heard the right answer to the question that you asked. You appear devious and feel slightly sleazy. 2: If the customers do not have an idea of what they want to spend, they will give you the maximum and stretch it all they want, because they are usually in the early stages of shopping and looking for somebody to give them the grand tour which "Money is no object" seems to deserve. You end up showing a couple of potential buyers everything that they don't need now but would like to have someday. And someday is when you'll make the sale. But today you worked for free. And the customer continues to shop.

So both responses to the cheap question are predictable, and one results in your selling less than you or the customer would have liked, and the other results in you selling nothing at all. That's just a couple of reasons why the cheap question is a cheap proposition, and feels like it.

Salespeople who have come from other price-competitive industries have often posed the following question to me: the customer says, soon after meeting you, "How much does all this stuff cost?" "Doesn't that warrant concern," they ask? The customer brought up the subject of price first, so shouldn't you confront it as an important issue?

My answer: if *you* do, it *will* be. What I mean by that is if you take the lead of the customer in this case, you will soon be looking at price as the most important, and quite possibly, only, concern. You'll be talking dollars and cents instead of features and ideas, and the customer can get that kind of conversation from any one of your competitors. When a person asks, "How much?" simply answer his question. Tell him how much. If he doesn't frown or tell you he wants to look at something else, you can assume that you have his approval to continue with the sales process. Responding to the customer's, "How much does it cost?" with, "How much do you want to spend?" sounds about the same as your responding to, "How do you feel?" with, "How do I look like I feel?" That's an exchange of words rather than a communication.

Does one cheap question deserve so much attention? *Yes.* It's a critical point of departure, a juncture that will have you pitting strategy on one hand or practicing communicating on the other, and it's awkward if not debilitating, to do both at the same time. It's not easy to do something *to* somebody and *with* somebody at the same time and feel as though it were a mutual endeavor. It is also interesting to note that every time I've placed less emphasis on this point, there is always one salesperson who is so steadfast in his belief that the cheap question is the key to sales success and riches, that I end up spending even more time than normal addressing this issue. It's not easy to give up a bad habit which so many other people still indulge. "But so-and-so says it all the time, and look at him," says the salesperson, in defense of what seems to be a short-cut and is actually a giant detour.

If I have the opportunity to look at so-and-so, I can assure you that if that salesperson would throw away the crutch of the cheap question, he would not only sell more than he already does, but sell it more profitably and assure himself a giant increase in repeat business. When you ask the customer about price before product, it's not too hard to figure out what your priority is. And what you can do for a person as far as price is concerned is not controlled by you. A good deal is not always yours to make. And that's the main reason for so-and-so getting any repeat business. The store, your marketing department, the manufacturers, supply and demand, devaluation or inflation of the dollar, the national economy and virtually everything else but you determines your control over price and ability to give another super deal.

This business—the CE business, your business—is competitive. But the competition is in the nature of the equipment and services offered. How competitive you are depends upon selection of product; how the customer feels because of how your store is merchandised; what you can offer the customers in the form of services beyond a discount (doesn't everybody do that?); where your store is located; what kind of message you send to the customer; and, most important, you. YOU, as I said much earlier on, are the way to get the edge on the competition. You and the service which you provide are the reason why the customer chooses to shop at one store over another. How you treat the customer makes the real difference. You are the reason the customer shops more than once at the same store. The competitive nature of this business does not hinge on price as much as blazing newsprint and red tag sales would lead you to believe. A recent industry study showed that less than twenty percent of total customers on a regular business day (excluding special events) are "ad" customers. If you talk to twelve customers on days when you are doing your regular advertising, you can assume on an averaged basis that only two or three of those people are in the store because of a specially advertised "deal." The other nine people are there because of all of the reasons that we have already talked about.

A recent industry research report published figures that said that the average business can blame *price* for less than ten percent of their customer turnover. The greatest percentage of customers are lost because of indifferent and inattentive salespeople. Remember what I said about bad news traveling fast, and also about how good an impression you have to make if you're going to be someone worth talking about. Well, that same phenomenon distorts our perception of the customers that we do business with. You remember the good customers, and they make your drive home worthwhile. But you also remember the customers who were only interested in price, and they keep you awake at night. You stay awake trying to figure what you did wrong, or why that burned-out price-conscious shopper had to ruin a good day. Though your concern is commendable, it is actually a waste of time. As long as you've been doing what we've been talking about, you've done nothing wrong. But I'll tell you who did. *It was the salesperson with the cheap question who had to shoot a cheap price to save face which made a cruiser out of a customer and a shopper out of your buyer.* Most people who are fixated by price are given their free orientation course in discounting and price wars by salespeople who have no use for sales techniques. They just keep shaking and nodding their heads and thinking, "What the customer doesn't know won't hurt 'em or help 'em."

People generally respond to what they're asked with some degree of continuity. Ask a person about price enough times and his response will be predictable—and keep you awake at night because you are too apt to remember the bad experiences which only account for a slim margin of your business. It's hard to rationalize what appears to be a total lack of sensitivity. But forget about the bad news customer. We've all had our bad days and outrageous moments. Move on, and recall the things that went right for you. Seek instruction in your most positive moments; find your support by remembering the customers who made your day, and guess what? You'll go to sleep a lot faster, because there's more to think about when you concentrate on the positive aspects of selling or of anything else for that matter. The customers who make your job worthwhile outnumber the other ones four-to-one. I've always insisted that you don't let the eccentric ten percent of your business ruin the other positive ninety percent. It doesn't take a course in negotiation for you to figure out why that's a good deal. It's just good sense and good *business* sense as well.

If you make sure that you're prepared for your customers, and meet them with mutual satisfaction as your goal, and make a sincere and concentrated effort to find out their needs, you will find yourself presenting the right equipment at the right price with the right attitude. Customers carry around foggy estimates of how much they should spend after adding up prices out of newspapers and inserts and recalculating the total based on wishful thinking about how much something should cost.

By being an expert listener and being able to respond with the information and ideas which you have at your command, you'll get a better and more accurate perception of what the customer wants and should spend, than by asking them outright. Confirming what they believe to be a fact—which is often an opinion without much research—is one of the reasons they came to you. They need you to tell them how right or wrong, how close or far-off they may be—they need you! Remember that—it's a matter of your self-respect. It's something to feel good about. The customer is your professional responsibility. If you believe it, you'll soon find yourself standing in front of people who respect you for what you're doing. They'll be waiting for you to show them how to buy what you have so accurately perceived as being right for them. You don't need a cheap question when the answer is a matter of communicating with someone who needs you.

Asking and Answering
Buying Questions

The Time to Confirm a Good First Impression

I'VE TALKED ABOUT the cheap question, but before getting to
the final step of the sale, I want you to consider some other
questions which are anything but cheap. These are the buying
questions that are a result of the worthwhile idea you presented in a sterling fashion. One type of buying question is
something that the *customer* will ask, and the other type is
something that *you* will ask the customer. In both cases, these
questions will assist you in making the sale, while also making
it a more profitable experience for both you and your customer.

Before addressing buying questions specifically, I want
to make sure that you are aware of the importance of the
customer's perception at this point in the sale—which is near
the end of your presentation and approaching the time of the
customer's purchase. The customer knows that the time for
making a decision is getting closer, so the customer may come
up with reasons to put off doing what he wants to do (for very
understandable reasons that I will talk about when you get to
the next step). It is therefore important for you to look every
bit as good as you did when you first greeted the customer.
You want to confirm the customer's good first impression. The
best way of doing this is not to comb your hair again, smile

harder, or realign your eye contact. The way to confirm the customer's good first impression while also reaffirming the fact of the purchase, is to continue to pay special attention to the customer.

During the presentation, you have the opportunity to talk more. You have the chance to inform the customer and clarify the idea of the purchase, to answer questions and make a button really worth pushing. But don't get so verbal that the customer doesn't have a chance to say: "Yes." "What did you say?" I've actually heard salespeople ask customers that. The customer says, "Okay, I'll take it," and the salesperson is still listening to his or her own commentary, and upon hearing a faint affirmation in the background, slams on the brakes and says, "What'd you say?" "I said wrap it up," the customer replies.

Asking Buying Questions and Selling Accessories

So don't get too carried away...keep listening. The last moment you want the customers to have to clarify something is when they say, in so many words, "I'll take it." Pay special attention to the customers by asking them to get involved with the equipment, by asking them to push an eject button and see how smoothly a particular mechanism works, by asking them to find the right channel, or by handing the remote control to them and telling them how to use it.

If you're demonstrating a portable or a personal stereo, make sure that the customer has the headphones on his head and the unit in his hand so he can feel how tiny and simple it is (or how big and fancy it is—depending on what idea you're selling).

Or, when you're demonstrating a turntable or CD player, tell your customer how to cue up a record or CD, and then let her do it. The customer who experiences the equipment in the store will probably be experiencing the equipment in his or her home faster than the customer who was made to feel that *Don't Touch* was your store policy. And, of course, when you're getting the customers in touch with the equipment, you are paying special attention to them—you are making sure that they do it right. They know you still care. They know you're still there and didn't give them up for the sound of your own voice.

You should also listen for opportunities to ask the customers questions that will momentarily have them considering owning or using the equipment. Get them accustomed to ownership by asking buyer questions that express what you have believed all along: that the customers are going to buy today because they are looking for the satisfaction that can only come with a purchase. Buyer questions ask the customers to think about the things that will happen when they take the equipment home, hook the equipment up, or while they are using the equipment. In all cases, you are asking about things that the customers must consider after taking ownership. Things like:

"Do you think fifteen foot speaker cables will be long enough?"

"How often will you be recording programs?"

"About how much tape do you think you'll be using per month?"

"How often do you think you'll be recording programs versus playing pre-recorded tapes?"

"What kind of tape will you be using most often—hi-bias or normal?"

"Will you be putting the speakers on shelves or are you going to need speaker stands?"

"How often will you be renting pre-recorded tapes?"

When your customers answer any of these questions, they not only have to consider themselves as owners previous to the invoice, but, given the focus of most of the buying questions, the are also being introduced to some important accessories at the right time during the sale (rather than taking an approach dreaded by most consumers, "Adding up" the extras at the end of the sale and waiting to see "What it comes out to.''). When you show the customers speaker cables, speaker stands, tapes, and head cleaners, they will have already acknowledged the need for these items. Accessories are to be presented *within the flow of the sale,* rather than *at the end of the sale* . . . one last move that can get the customers out of the buying mood just a few moments before they were going to say, ''We'll take it.''

Accessories should also be presented as maintenance items to the CE customer. Everything that you call an accessory is something that your customers need if they want good sound or a good picture. The accessories that the CE salesperson sells are not just things that would be nice to have—they are things that you *have* to have if you want optimum performance—and isn't that the only kind of performance that deserves to follow the magic sell? So don't be shy in your presentation of accessories.

It's difficult to appreciate a new system if the stylus has to rake its way through the grimy grooves of a neglected record. It's pretty hard to get excited about the fantastic dynamic range of a CD recording if the bass got lost in the carpet before reaching your ears. And it's impossible to record something without tape. Yet it is amazing, and especially perplexing, how many CE customers get a cassette deck home and find themselves without tape. (So off they scurry to the closest drugstore to buy the low-bias three-for-a-buck-ninety-eight special.) And you can't blame them for not asking to buy the tape. They may have assumed there was at least one in the box. After all, there was when they bought their sixty-dollar portable—but now they find there wasn't one included with their new four-hundred dollar three-head three-motor dream machine.

If you ask the right buyer question, you'll remind yourself to hand the customers a case of tape with their deck and they'll be ready to accept it as something they need. Accessories can also help you build some of the profit back into an advertised item or systems. And the more boxes—big or small—that the customer carries out the door, the more excited and the more satisfied they're going to feel.

So pay close attention to the customer while you're

presenting the idea of the equipment and you'll be doing both yourself and your customer a favor. It's in the spirit of the magic sell. Whenever you make somebody else feel good, you feel good, too. And customers are waiting for your ideas and your suggestions. If you don't give them the right idea and if don't have any suggestions, they may take it as a sign that you don't care, or that you've given up on them as buyers—just when they needed your support, suggestions, and enthusiasm the most. The motivators that make the sale happen are your responsibility. Don't let the customers down now . . . just because they started glancing down at their feet and then at each other, fidgeting, and starting to say something and then deciding not to. Stay with them, maintain your dignity and pay attention—pretty soon they'll be breathing an audible sigh of relief and looking at you with smiling and excited expressions that tell you everything you've been wanting to hear all along.

Answering Buying Questions

In addition to getting the customer in touch with the equipment and asking buying questions to suggest the needed accessories, there is another way of paying special attention to your customer which is also very much to your advantage. And it's just a matter of listening. Sometimes when customers start to buy the idea, it is hard for them to conceal their desire to own what they have just perceived so vividly. They will ask *you* buyer questions. These are questions that have something to do with buying the equipment, hooking it up, or using it, except now the customer is doing the asking. Things like:

C: Do you carry your own financing?
S: We sure do. And we also have a ninety-days-same-as-cash option which I'd like to tell you about.

C: How hard is it to hook this stuff up?
S: It's really pretty simple. Here, let me draw you a diagram that will make hooking it up a snap.

C: Do you deliver?

S: Yes we do. When would you like it to be delivered?

C: What other colors does it come in?

S: Quite a few. What color were you thinking of buying?

When your customers asks these types of questions, they are actually telling you that they want to buy. So it's really very easy for you to answer their questions because, if you're listening closely, you know that you've already sold them on the idea. Other buying questions that your customers may ask include, "Is there a manual that explains everything?" or ,"I could always buy the back two speakers later, couldn't I?" or, "Do you carry the jacks and cords and everything I'll need to install it?" or, "How many do you have in stock?"

Buying questions are the most positive thing you can hear, and the best way to pay special attention to your customer at this point in the sale. Just make sure you hear them.

And remember to ask them.

STEP SEVEN
The Magic Sell as It Happens

Attaining Mutual Satisfaction
With the Magic Sell

THE CUSTOMERS THAT YOU'RE LISTENING TO have been in the store for almost an hour. Right now they're trying to decide on whether they would like the smaller two-way speakers, or the larger three-ways. Everything else has been decided. They want the seventy-five watt stereo/video receiver, the turntable with the new super Trans-Nine cartridge, the most fully-featured CD player that you carry, the Eon dubbing cassette deck which does everything but clean its own heads, and they said they wanted the special speaker cables that you told them was as much a part of the speaker as the crossover... you liked that line. (It really did seem to give them the idea of how high-performance speaker cables add to the quality of the sound.)

You presented the cartridge in a similar manner. And that's right—mustn't forget the record cleaning kit which they also wanted. "A dirty record can make a good system sound bad," you told them. "But a properly cleaned record can make a good system sound great." A good way of putting it, you had to admit. They really got the idea.

The wife now turns and says to you, "Ray, you know what our room is like. Don't you think the smaller speakers would be fine for that room?"

"Yes," you reply. "They'd sound great, and of course the contoured oak cabinets would complement the decor of any room."

"Yeah Ray, we know that," says the husband. "But as long as we're doing it, we might as well do it right. I mean, I don't plan on buying a new system every other year. That's why I'm wondering whether the three-ways might not just be a better choice."

"Well Ron, the receiver that you're buying is certainly capable of driving the larger speakers to the maximum. And like you mentioned, when Patti is away, you're going to want to turn up the volume and listen to some of those old favorites of yours. And your old favorites don't exactly fall into the easy-listening category. Which is not to say that the Ref E's won't play loud, but if you want a really impressive bass response, you'd probably be more satisfied with the larger speakers over the long run."

"But Ron—"

"Patti, listen to what the man is saying."

"Patti, both speakers are very nice. Remember when we played Barbara Streisand, and you said that it was better than hearing her on stage? Well, that was when we were listening to the Towers. It's the mid-range speaker—the one that the Ref E's don't have—and that extremely accurate tonal balance which enables the Towers to capture the subtle qualities of the human voice and reproduce it so perfectly. A soprano will never be mistaken for a contralto. But it's you're decision, and I want you both to be happy.

However, given your individual tastes, I get the feeling that both of you would be happier with the Towers. You get everything that the Ref E's have and much more. They're good-looking speakers, they sound better than anything else in the room, and the longer you live with them, the more you're going to like them."

"Okay Ray, you're probably right," says the wife. "And you certainly know more about this stuff than either of us."

You smile, and Ron puts his arm around Patti who is smiling after making the final decision. "Ray," says Ron, "give us one of your cards."

You hear him say it, but you can't believe it. You've heard it before, but you just didn't expect it this time. "My

*card?" you ask with an expression that only reveals a hint of
the shock and disappointment which you feel.*

*"Yeah, your card or something, so that I can add up
what all this stuff is going to cost me."*

*You recover quickly, and escort Ron and Patti to the
closest desk calculator.*

*"It's a lot of money, but I suppose it's worth it if it'll
make her happy," Ron says, looking at Patti after getting the
total.*

*"What do you mean? Make me happy? Look at you
smiling like a big kid. Ray, let me just pay for this, so I can get
him out of here."*

*They're both laughing, and you have that Saturday
feeling again. It's not just making a sale; it's being part of a
happy event. It's making other people happy as well as yourself.*

It's mutual satisfaction. The magic sell just happened.

* * *

That's the way it's supposed to happen, and the way it
will most of the time, if you follow all the steps which I've
talked about. Because, you see, there are really only six steps
to the magic sell. The seventh one is when it happens.

I'm sure that you've already figured out that "closing" a
sale starts before you say a word to the customer—before you
even say "Hi." That's pretty logical, don't you think? Why
would we bother tuning up our attitude, and going through
some pretty thorough preparatory steps if it didn't have
something to do with making the sale? And what is the goal of
the magic sell? You're right—mutual satisfaction. That's why
you made sure that you were getting through to the customer,
and doing something that a lot of other salespeople take for
granted and never really do accomplish—listening and communicating. When it came to the equipment, you gave them
the right ideas and turned the mystery into magic. You made
certain your customers understood that they had made a good
choice. You wanted them to be satisfied and you wanted to
feel the same way.

Why "Thinking It Over" Is Really Not the Idea

It's appropriate here to mention that "satisfy" is just a better way of saying "closing." The expression "closing" insinuates that you are finalizing the sale (which you are), but it does not allow for much of anything to happen after the sale is finalized. Whenever you close a sale, you should think about opening up another one. One sale should lead to another one—either with the customer who has just purchased something from you or with someone whom that customer knows. A satisfied customer will make sure that happens. Think about the last time you felt such a sense of satisfaction as a consumer that you felt like telling somebody about it. Would you have felt that kind of satisfaction without buying something? Of course not. And was the salesperson who had made the sale also talking about it? Probably so. Why? Because the salesperson felt as good about it as you. Buying or selling something is the only way a customer or a salesperson can find satisfaction (because of mutual satisfaction) in a CE store. So if you talk about, "Closing a customer," think about "Satisfying a customer," and you will be looking forward to new sales as well as acknowledging the sale that just happened.

And sometimes something else happens before the sale. It's happened to all of us at one time or another. Take yourself off the sales floor for a moment . . . you're on the dance floor, and the rhythm of the music and the movements of you and your partner's body have merged to create a kind of harmony that's music all by itself. Then you miss a beat, or your foot comes down wrong, and suddenly your exquisite timing, balance and movement falls apart in a flurry of embarrassment and disappointment.

The same thing can happen when you're selling. A wrong move, a product that decides to buzz at the wrong time, something that was in stock that somebody else sold before your customers made a decision, a slip of the tongue, drawing a blank instead of the line that counts . . . these are all things that can disrupt your focus or concentration. But by making a genuine effort to do everything that I have talked about-. . . not just one of the steps or part of a step that sounded good to you . . . but by practicing all six steps, you will find that, by no coincidence, fewer of these "unexpected" things will occur to prevent that seventh step from happening just as magically as it should.

Too many things on the sales floor are shrugged off as being out of your control, *but you have control over more than you think.* Start by recognizing the importance of the five P's that we discussed in step one: *proper planning prevents poor performance.* Now let me add PPR—which doesn't stand for perfect public relations, but could well assist you in approaching that as one of your goals. PPR stands for Prepare, Practice, and Refine. And that takes us up to where we are in step seven. Not only should you prepare with the five P's in mind, and practice listening techniques on your friends before putting them into practice with every customer, but you should also take the time to refine those techniques. They will give the movements of the selling process that same sense of excitement, balance and mutual coordination that you feel when you're dancing with the right person.

But there's also the time when you're dancing with someone who looks at someone else across the floor, or remembers something that has nothing to do with the music, or doubts his or her ability to follow you into the move that will turn a few heads, and suddenly you feel as if you're dancing by yourself—and you might as well be, unless you can do something to revitalize the other person or restore his or her lost confidence.

Does something like that ever happen when you're selling?

For a moment, it appeared that it was going to happen with Ron and Patti and it didn't feel too good, did it? Given the intensity of the sales relationship which you manage to affect—getting to know the other person so well in such a short amount of time as you near a mutually worthwhile objective—being told, "I'd rather not...at least, not right now," can be a pretty sudden letdown. Enough to take your breath away for a moment or two. You might even find yourself at a loss for words.

You want to listen, but finding yourself speechless is obviously not the way. So how do you handle this situation that can sometimes occur, regardless of how well prepared and practiced you may be? How do you turn a moment of indecision into an affirmative action? How do you find the momentum that was there one moment and gone the next?

If you don't make the attempt to repair broken lines of communication, and readjust feelings in order to reach agreed upon objectives, you are saying something to yourself about yourself that I don't think you want to hear. You are saying that you never cared in the first place, that customers, i.e., people, are expendable, that relationships are fine as long as everything is going fine, but hear a murmur of dissatisfaction or see a ripple of discontent, and it's disappearing time. There's nothing magic about a disappearing act when you're selling or when your building any other kind of interpersonal relationship. And you are not the kind of person who thinks this way.

How do I know? Very simple—you wouldn't be reading this book at this point if you felt that way. Our values and goals are similar, otherwise you would have already left in search of the magic pill or gone back to doing everything the way you were doing it before you started reading these pages.

You are the kind of person who feels that people are worth your time, and have unique needs. Upon discovering those needs, you then feel that it is as much your responsibility as theirs to see that those needs are satisfied. You're not standing with the customer beside a magic fountain with a handful of coins ready to make a couple dozen wishes. You're standing with the customer in a magical environment called a CE store, in front of some devices that will produce their own kind of magic that you can hear and see. And the customers are standing with a person who is aware of that magic feeling—that feeling good is the only way you should ever leave a CE store. You know that if you can make it happen for the customer, you can make it happen for yourself. Otherwise, you're wasting your time and—worse—you're leading the customer on.

Think of the person who you would like to be with most right now. Get his or her image well set in your mind. Okay . . . you have the image. Now think about what you would do if that person told you right now—in person or by telephone— that he or she appreciates the time you've spent, but right now would just as soon go his or her own way just to think things over. The person is unsure of a lot of things, and just needs to get away and talk things over with some other people. How would that be? Would you mind? Would you say something or do something if I could further assure you that there was a better than seventy percent chance that the other person would never get back in touch with you?

Of course you would. And for similar reasons, you would bother to correct a problem between you and the customer that takes a turn towards the drastic—when you recognize the words, "Could I have your card?" or, "I'd just like to think it over," as being almost equivalent to, "See you around sometime." The end result will be pretty much the same if you hand over your card or open the door for them to go mull it over. The chances are good that the person will keep on putting off what he or she wants to do, or eventually buy something similar to what you have presented to them from somebody else, which doesn't mean much in the way of satisfaction for you. And there's nothing too "mutual" about that.

Even though that's what the person will most likely do, that's probably not what the person is consciously thinking of doing when he or she says, "I'd like to think it over." And, of course, this is to your advantage—if you respond appropriately. But before talking about that, let me give you a list of several phrases that you will hear that all mean pretty much the same thing:

> "I'd like to take some time and think it over."

> "I'd like to talk it over with my wife (or husband)."

> "Let me sleep on it. . . . "

> "Like I told you, this is the first place we've been too."

> "I'd like to talk it over with my friend, and maybe bring him in, too."

> "I've really got to check my finances before making a final decision."

"I have to wait until we're sure about the new house (or until I get my tax refund, or until I find out about the new job, or, until my daughter comes home for her vacation, or until the settlement comes through, or until payday, or . . .*until I feel strongly enough about the idea of the equipment to take action and buy it and make it my own*)."

Each of these phrases are just ways of saying, "No—not right now—maybe later." So for purposes of understanding what to do in order to satisfy the objective of the magic sell, consider, "I'd like to think it over," as the all-inclusive statement which you have to handle now if step seven is going to happen. And, of course, if you were practicing steps one through six to make seven happen, it means, conversely, that if step seven doesn't happen now, there wasn't much justification for practicing the other six.

In all cases, the customers are asking you to be patient, to wait for them to make up their minds; which seems like a perfectly reasonable request. It is . . . if your objective was anything other than what it is. The customer came to you wanting to buy something, otherwise he or she would have left before now. The customer would not have spent this much of his or her time, or this much of your time, if he or she had just been window shopping.

As a matter of fact, most people don't like to take this much of a person's time unless they are serious about making a purchase. That's a fair assumption that you can prove by your own experience. How often do you have enough free time or feel perverse enough to enter a store and spend over fifteen minutes asking questions and talking about something unless you have a sincere desire to buy whatever it is you're talking about? After talking with the salesperson, you may find a reason to put off buying. But if you wanted to buy something and the salesperson did everything that we have so far talked about and you decided not to buy, what would be the most probable reason?

Money? Not really. You probably would not be talking to someone at the store if affording "it" was out of the question. You'd still be staring at that special page in an insert, or telling friends and family that someday you're gonna buy such-and-such, just to get their reactions and find out just how real your buying intentions were.

Perhaps "it" didn't look as you imagined it. That's not an acceptable reason; the salesperson would have found out your expectations and addressed your needs and presented an alternative.

Maybe it cost more than you thought it was going to. No, not really; the salesperson would have found out what you wanted and by step five would have made certain that there were no dollar surprises littering the approach to the purchase. You may have even decided on a credit purchase versus cash, or gone so far as to put it on layaway. If you could afford it enough to come in and talk about it, the salesperson could find a way for you to be a buyer rather than an embarrassed shopper.

Maybe you needed a second opinion, after all. But that's not really an acceptable reason, either. You would probably feel that your own opinion was good enough if the salesperson had adequately endorsed your choice and reinforced your idea of yourself as a smart buyer and good decision-maker.

Maybe the store just didn't feel right. But if the salesperson was prepared and could communicate to you that the biggest value in the store was his or her services, the store *would* feel right. Think about where you've made some of your fondest purchases. The place wasn't always merchandised like Neiman-Marcus was it?

So what's left? Something very real, and something you must understand and relate to if you are going to make step seven happen. It's something that you experience along with almost every other retail customer before making the purchase. *It's called being sensible. It's called using good sense.* It's your not going off half-cocked on some crazy shopping spree. It's your not just throwing your money away. That's an act reserved for monarchs, musicians who just got their first gold record, and movie stars who fall in love in public. You may live in a free-enterprise system, but you were also touched at one time or another by a puritan ethic that influenced how you buy things. ("Don't spend it all in one place," is a phrase with a serious origin. "Don't buy the first thing you see," is advice to curb the buying impulse in us all. "Do you really need it?" is a question that has slowed us all down at one time or another.)

This early influence has produced a buying pattern that has survived a couple of wars, the sixties revolution, the "Me" generation, and is now back in vogue with the baby-boom generation. Symptoms include sweaty hands before buying something that you really don't need—like a pair of running shoes that you found in this great new color when you already have a pair that has enough tread for ten consecutive marathons. Or self-doubt when buying someone a special present when you were planning on making a token purchase . . . you know, when you realize that it's really not just the thought that counts. Or nagging guilt as you notate the check in your register and you're still telling yourself that it's not too late to ask for your check back. Or a quickening pulse and fast breathing when you start saying things to yourself like, "If I don't do it now, I never will," or, "What difference is a hundred dollars going to make a year from now?"

These are all symptoms of our "good sense" working on us when we want to enjoy the money we have worked for, and do something foolish like spending it!

It is essential that you recognize this inhibiting influence on the customer's purchase. If you don't, you'll find yourself expressing the same attitude—or empathizing with this same vague reason for not buying something. And soon you'll be unselling the customer on what you just sold them. When something good was just about to happen, you both agree, for reasons that are bigger than both of you, that it would be a bad thing, after all. People take the same rationale they apply to other moral decisions in their lives that deserve it, and apply it to a buying decision that doesn't deserve it. And it happens as frequently in a CE store as in any retail establishment on the block.

Remember, the very thing that gives your environment a magical feeling is also the thing that can make your environment a tough place to make good decisions. Luxury devices that provide people with pure pleasure and enjoyment without practical justification other than "We deserve it," can make for a tough sell. You must be aware of this attitude, which is a product of this country's history...otherwise you'll find yourself sympathizing with it because it's part of your background, too.

> C: I like it. In fact, I think it's great, but maybe it's just not the right time.
> S: The right time?
> C: Yeah, I was just sort of planning on looking around when I came in, and then before I knew it, I got to talking to you about a new television and for a while it seemed like a good idea, but now I don't know.
> S: I can understand how you feel. The new TV monitors are pretty amazing, and when you watch something in stereo for the first time...
> C: Yeah, that's the whole deal right there. I come in and *wow*, before I know it, I'm watching old Skywalker scramble around in the snow, and pretty soon I'm ready to buy out the whole store and my wife doesn't even know where I am. Which brings up a good point—I better get home or I'm gonna miss dinner and everybody's gonna be mad at dear old dad.
> S: It's pretty easy to tell the difference between a conventional TV and the more advanced sets, especially with real high fidelity sound.
> C: You're telling me! Hey listen, why don't you give me your card, and maybe I'll drop by on a weekend or something, okay?
> S: Sure thing. Here's my card.

It's *not* a sure thing. Just as we all share the same reasons for buying things, we all share the same reasons for not buying things. And your job is to find a way for people to buy things. Can you remember anything that you almost bought that you'd love to have now but is currently on the low priority list? You ever hear yourself saying, "I could kick myself for not buying..." and then launch into a description of something that everybody would want to own if they "had any sense at all."

Well, don't blame yourself. Now you're saying you should have bought if you had used your good sense. But when the item was available, your "good sense" prevailed and the salesperson's didn't. The salesperson is to blame for not showing you that sometimes the time is right when it doesn't seem like it. You don't want to have people out there blaming you for not motivating them to buy what they could be enjoying now. Instead, you want to have people saying, "If that person hadn't been such a great salesperson, I'd still be looking at a green picture and listening to a speaker that wouldn't make it in the backseat of my car." Don't let all of the good reasons you just gave the person for buying something get lost in the dust of a hasty departure. (Remember, there is nothing magic about a disappearing act.)

Instead, make sure they get to experience the good things that you sell—and which you sell because you believe they're worth buying:

> C: I like it. In fact, I think it's great, but maybe it's just not the right time.
> S: The right time?
> C: Yeah, I was just sort of planning on looking around when I came in, and then, before I knew it, I got to talking to you about a new television and for a while it seemed like a good idea, but now I don't know.
> S: I understand how you feel. Recently I went in with a friend to help pick out a new car. He didn't buy one, but there's a brand new van with a sunroof and mag wheels out there in that parking lot that belongs to me. Once I saw it, I knew I wanted it. I knew the family and I were going to have one of the best vacations we'd ever had. We're going to drive up to the lake this weekend, and then take a trip up to Glacier on my vacation. We haven't been able to use it for anything more than around-town driving yet, but already it's provided us with more pleasure than I would have imagined when I bought it. I didn't know whether I was doing the right thing when I bought it, but I know now.
>
> Given what you told me about your current television, I think you'd be doing more people than just yourself a favor by buying something that you immediately recognized as a good idea. Because it *is* a good idea.

C: You got a good point, but right now—oh, *wow* (glancing at his watch)—you got any idea what time it is? I better get home or I'm gonna miss dinner and everybody's gonna be mad at dear old dad. You got a card? I'll stop in and see you this weekend.

S: I sure do, but you just brought up a pretty good point yourself. You were enjoying yourself so much and got so involved in the new monitor that you lost track of time. Give me just a minute to explain, and I'll show you how you can be late for dinner and be a hero at the same time. In fact, you might just make this a night that the whole family will remember the rest of their lives as something really special.

C: I think I know what you've got in mind.

S: You did say that you and your wife had talked about getting a new TV soon, right?

C: Right.

S: Well let's consider tonight.

The salesperson will not only sell a new television monitor, but will enrich the customer's life with an experience that the customer and his family will be talking about every time someone mentions that they have a new TV.

The magic sell is the sale that everybody talks about long after it happened; it's almost like a vacation in that it's a good memory that you can call on to brighten up your day or to feel even better about somebody you consider special. "Dad's big surprise" will now be family legend, and always be remembered with affection. But Dad had to take a little bit of a chance and ride a dare to make a good idea something worth talking about for a long time.

The salesperson's method of finalizing the sale is something we will talk about a little bit later on. But for now, note that that wasn't an "easy close," it was just highly effective—personally inspired and creative. That's how you make what people want to happen, really happen!

Don't, to any degree, let the message here get lost in your translation. Being prudent, investing your money wisely, and saving money because it gives a person a measure of financial security is everybody's personal concern. That is not a decision you will ever have to make for a person. The only time you have to help a person make a decision with regard to their finances, and the only time you have to give a person the confidence to do what he wants to do, is after he has spent minutes or hours or days, after repeated visits, and after he has said *this is what I want* and *this is what I need.* When the seventh step comes around, you have to be there to give the encouragement and provide the justification for letting him buy something that he's told you he wants.

That is fundamental to your job as a salesperson. Your job is not to say, "Hi," ask insightful questions, listen with an astute ear, present the wonderfully simple and exciting idea of an otherwise pretty complicated piece of hardware, and then leave it up to the customer's discretion to buy or not to buy. That's called presenting with a personal touch. It's also called working for free. It's not selling.

Selling is when you deserve to be paid for your energy and talent. Selling is finding a way for the seventh step—*the magic sell*—to happen. Selling is assuring the customer that with your help, he or she will be able to own what they've dreamed about. There's something truly magical about that.

I posed a situation earlier that concerned a favorite person of yours telling you to go away and come back later. I asked how you would feel and what you would do about it, in order to emphasize the importance of addressing the customer's need to buy, rather than passing it off as, "Another day in the life . . . " and turning over your card.

Right now, let's turn down the drama and look at another couple and a common occurrence in everybody's life.

The weekend is coming up and the husband and wife have talked about visiting some friends who have moved to another town. He's really looking forward to it. He even made some preparations. He got the car washed, and bought a nice bottle of wine. He also has a new album that he's planning on taking along.

His wife, who, he thought, was anticipating this as much

as he, says that it's been an exhausting week, and she would rather stay home and relax if it's alright with him.

What do you think would happen if the husband said: "Tough. We're going to see Ali and Bill anyway?" The husband would probably go by himself, or stay home and relax— whether he feels like it or not. What if he said: "Would you please go—just for me?" The husband probably wouldn't be much better off. Or what if the husband said, "Do you know how much trouble I've gone to, and how much I've looked forward to this? And now all for nothing? I mean, show a little consideration?" The husband would probably still stay home—except now he's admitted that he's a selfish jerk.

In all of the above responses he's looking out for number one—thinking strictly of yours truly.

What if he decided to spend a little effort communicating, and give his wife a couple of good reasons why he wants to visit friends and why he thinks she would enjoy it as well— rather than trying to get his way in twenty-five words or less?

What would the husband really say? He might start by saying something like: "We've stayed home for the last two weeks, and it might be nice to get out and have some fun with people we haven't seen for a long time."

And his wife replies: "You see new people every day; besides, last week we went to the movies and went out to dinner, and you bought two new albums. And you said we should do it more often."

"It was a great weekend," he agrees. "It really was. I remember saying that I didn't really care about seeing anybody but you if we could always spend time like that together. It was a great movie, and the sushi was terrific, and the Robert Cray album is a really great album. But the best thing about the whole weekend was you. I love to watch you laugh like you did in the theater . . . I love to watch you, period."

"You're really sweet sometimes, you know that? So why don't we do it this weekend if you loved it so much?" she asks.

"I think it would be great, but Bill called last week for the second time and asked us to come up, and it's really not that long of a drive. And I've got a great idea . . . we could take them up on their offer to stay over, get up the next day and on the way home have lunch at that little country inn that we've always talked about every time we go past. We'd have half the weekend to ourselves."

"It might be fun after all."

"Oh, and I forgot to tell you, they've got a pool at the new place and if the weather stays like this, it should really be a great weekend. You and Ali will end up telling jokes and trading book reviews and . . . "

"You and Bill will end up playing the music so loud I won't be able to hear myself think. What would I wear?" she asks.

"What about your new white pants or maybe your blue shorts, because if the weather. . . . " The wife will soon be anticipating the weekend as much as her husband. And it sounds as though it's going to be fun for both of them.

A pretty normal conversation, wouldn't you say? You've been part of similar ones on countless occasions. It's called *getting your way but not at the expense of the other person.* You can always do what you want—but enjoying it, and doing it with somebody who will make the experience even more pleasurable, is generally the idea. That's the idea of selling too, isn't it? In fact, that conversation is very similar to ones that you have during the last step of the sale.

You've presented a system to the customers, and have taken the time to show them how to hook it and shown them the cleaning devices and special speaker cables that you know they will need to make sure that it looks, sounds and works right. The customers have been nodding and smiling every step of the way. You know that they're going to buy it and really enjoy it. You're looking forward to it almost more than they are. You're about to ask how they wanted to pay for it, when the husband says, "I don't know, the more I think about it, the more I think we shouldn't just rush into this thing. Maybe we just need a little more time to think about it."

What would happen if you said, "Tough luck pal, you're buying whether you like it or not?" The customers would leave and, I hope—for the good of the industry—so would you. What if you said, "Would you please just go ahead and buy it right now? Just for me?" They would quickly understand whose best interests you had in mind. What if you said something that you've probably heard before: "I don't really understand why you need to think it over. After all, you've spent a lot of time, and I've shown you the best thing we have to offer. I just don't know what there is to think over?" Maybe you don't, but the customers certainly do—especially now. The customers are clear on one thing—that you don't understand.

But if you understand their response as something that can often happen at this time in the sale, you will let them know you understand by telling them so:

> S: I know exactly how you feel. Sometimes when something special is about to happen, something that you've anticipated, you start doubting the situation. Maybe it's because we spend so much energy thinking about it before it happens—I don't know, but anybody that's gotten married has experienced it. And that's probably the most important event of your life. Sometimes that moment of hesitation is good—it's your way of making sure that what is about to happen is right for you. Right now, it's your way of making sure that this system is going to provide as much enjoyment as you had expected.

> C: You got a real point. It's good to take the time and make sure you're doing the right thing. So why don't we get your card and we'll get back to you some time next week.

> S: Certainly. I will get you my card. Like I've told other customers who recognize the need to make a good decision—you want to make sure that you're going to enjoy the equipment you've chosen, and the best and only valid way of doing that is to set it up in your living room. Watch *The Empire Strikes Back* for the first time in real stereo without me standing next to you, hand the remote control to the kids and then as a family in the privacy of your own home think about it—the time and place to think about audio and video equipment is when you're listening and watching it. It's an experience that you have to see to believe —that's when you'll really know that you've done the right thing. I think I can say

with a fair degree of certainty that it is the right equipment for you, but you're the ones who have to prove it to yourselves.

The customers are now listening to every word you say, waiting for the phrase or words that will tell them that it's alright to do what they want. So you reinforce what they've almost done as if they had already done it—and they'll do it.

> S: And I know you're going to have a lot of enjoyment because you made the right decision and you bought what you wanted.

Probable replies from the customers might include statements like: "I think you're right," or, "Let's do it—we've talked about it long enough," or, "What are we waiting for, anyway?" or, "Do you take Visa?" Or the customers might ask, "What happens if it turns out not to be what we really want?"

There is usually a store refund or exchange policy to address that concern—which you rarely have to worry about. Because you're right—the customers have already given sufficient thought to making the purchase. It's time for the customers to make good on their promise to themselves, and enjoy themselves, and experience something new and exciting. They'll really know that they've done the right thing after they get the equipment home. And if you know that and believe it, tell it to the customers who are having some difficulty in finally making up their minds.

When the customers say, "Yes," in so many words, say, "Let me take you to the cashier's counter and you can get the paperwork out of the way, and then I want to give you a couple tips on using the record cleaner, and tell you about a couple other things that will keep the system performing like it should."

They now know that you won't disappear after they sign the invoice, and they are thinking about *using* the equipment rather than *buying* the equipment.

The Four Focal Points for the Seventh Step

When you sold the customer on the idea of the A/V system and when the husband sold his wife on the idea of a weekend away from home (and did it without intentionally using sales techniques), you both recognized the need to convey a positive mood to the other person which would work to your mutual advantage. You both sensed the need to communicate a sense of mutual excitement and anticipation, and thereby re-enthuse the other person about what you thought to be a very good idea. *And you both recognized an irony that reinforced the other person's self-esteem: when you have motivated the other person to say, "Yes," that person has made the decision, and not you.*

The same thing happened at the beginning of this chapter with Ron and Patti. Patti made the decision. And it happened again when the father decided to surprise his family with a new TV. The father felt that he made the decision—with the help of the salesperson's ability to create an exciting and memorable event —but it was the father who gave the go-ahead. If you "get your way" and feel good about it, it is with the *permission* of the other person and not in spite of, or at the expense of the other person.

But to do this, you must practice the techniques which we have talked about—you must listen, while utilizing a sense of control rather than venting your frustration or disappointment, and talk about what's being said rather than what's on your mind.

And use four focal points as guideposts for what you say:

1. ATTITUDE. Express an attitude or mood that makes doing what you would like to do more desirable and worthwhile to both of you. (Husband and Wife: The wife as the most important part of any weekend; laughter; fun; telling jokes and trading book reviews. Salesperson and Customer: Something special about to happen; anticipation; enjoyment; watching *E.*

Strikes Back in stereo with family in privacy of own home; equipment as an "experience.")

2. ALTERNATIVE. If necessary, be prepared to suggest attractive alternatives to your original plan. (H and W: Stay over and have lunch by themselves at a place they've talked about for a long time. S and C: Agreeing to give card and then convincing customer that being at home with the equipment is the place to think it over and prove to everyone that he had made the right decision.)

3. ADVANTAGES. *Always* emphasize the advantages to the other person of the action which you want to take or the alternative which you feel the need to suggest. (H and W: The swimming pool she didn't know about; just the two of them alone together for half the weekend. S and C: Making the purchase, and feeling that they are doing the right thing rather than having to still think about it.)

4. ACCESSORY. By focusing the other person's attention on accessory items or concerns, you will take the person from a decision mode ("Did I, or did I *not* do, the right thing?"), and instead have the person thinking about doing something like enjoying the equipment. (You will also make certain that you have sold the customers the things which make the system or component complete, and which also make the sale more profitable.) (H and W: The pool; the question of the wife's attire; and having lunch together on the way home. S and C: *E. Strikes Back* tape; remote control—even though it comes with component; record cleaner; additional maintenance advice.)

This is not a prescribed step-by-step method of finalizing sales, but the four focal points—a positive ATTITUDE, an attractive ALTERNATIVE, meaningful ADVANTAGES, and suitable ACCESSORIES—should guide your conversation. The four focal points will assist you in maintaining the right perspective for the seventh step.

You'll notice that there is some overlap in definition ... the attitude may also be the advantage or the advantage may also be the alternative, etc. That's the way it should be. Remember that these are focal points, and not a step-by-step method. If you're talking about or expressing any one of these four points during the seventh step, you will know that you are concerning yourself with the right things at the right time. One focal point might even seem to embody the other three, e.g., the alternative being a matter of attitude, advantages, and accessories. The four focal points can act as chords that strike the harmony for the seventh step.

To fully understand the importance of these four focal points, go back and review them for a moment and then try to imagine what the sale (or the weekend) would have felt like— or ask yourself whether it would have happened at all without the items noted in parenthesis which fall within the auspices of one or more of the four focal points. Go back to Ron and Patti and to the father who bought a video monitor rather than getting to the dinner table on time, and check to see when the salesperson uses the focal points.

The four focal points might be likened to the parallax marks in the viewfinder of a camera—stay within the marks and, given a properly maintained lens, you'll get the picture you wanted.

If you do get what you want at this point, you can also be assured that the customers are getting what they wanted. Sounds like mutual satisfaction doesn't it? You've made the purchase of a home entertainment device; an event that is exciting and worth talking about. Making the seventh step happen is the idea of the magic sell.

* * *

You have taken the time to fully prepare yourself for the CE customer and by following a seven-step approach, you have been able to effect worthwhile communications, discover and better define the customers' needs, and present the equipment while giving the customers an intelligent and irresistable idea of how they would personally use it. You have succeeded in building an accommodating and friendly ATTITUDE around the moment of the purchase. You had an ALTERNATIVE plan or choice of equipment, should the feelings or situation of the customers warrant it. You know the ADVANTAGES of making the purchase, and have made sure the customers also know. You have used ACCESSORIES as a way to complete the sale—as a way to make the purchase a special event.

And now your customers are looking forward to enjoying the equipment rather that questioning the act of spending money. You found that you were ready and willing to do something *for* the customers, rather than falling into a funk at the customers' first hesitation and ending up thinking about doing things *to* the customers out of a sense of desperation. You were aware of the tendency of customers to always want a little more time to think about something that they've thought about and put off doing for too long. Now the customers are smiling and shaking your hand, and now you give them your card and tell them to give you a call if they have the slightest problem with hooking it up, or if they have any questions at all. You tell them that you would like to think of this as just the beginning of a good relationship—they'll be needing tape, and cleaning fluid, and if they want you to give them a call when that new two-line speaker phone comes in, you'll be glad to do it. They say the things I told you they would say, and you smile and have a very good feeling deep inside as you watch the customers leave. It's almost like saying goodbye to two good friends.

The magic sell is yours, my friend.